DEVON AND CORNWALL RECORD SOCIETY

Extra Series 3

WILLIAM BIRCHYNSHAW'S MAP OF EXETER, 1743

Richard Oliver, Roger Kain and Todd Gray

Devon and Cornwall Record Society

The Boydell Press

First published 2019

A publication of the
Devon and Cornwall Record Society
published by The Boydell Press
an imprint of Boydell & Brewer Ltd
PO Box 9, Woodbridge, Suffolk IP12 3DF, UK
and of Boydell & Brewer Inc.
668 Mt Hope Avenue, Rochester, NY 14620–2731, USA
website: www.boydellandbrewer.com

ISBN 978 0 90185 397 4

Series information is printed at the back of this volume

A CIP catalogue record for this book is available
from the British Library

The publisher has no responsibility for the continued existence or accuracy
of URLs for external or third-party internet websites referred to in this book,
and does not guarantee that any content on such websites is,
or will remain, accurate or appropriate.

This publication is printed on acid-free paper

In memory of William Ravenhill,
author of a number of pathfinding studies of Exeter's maps

CONTENTS

ILLUSTRATIONS

CBTM refers to the Catalogue of British Town Maps at https://townmaps.history.ac.uk/

TABLES

BIRCHYNSHAW'S MAP

On 12 September 2018, Lot 333 was offered for sale at Bearnes Hampton & Littlewood, Exeter auctioneers. It comprised a framed map of Exeter and was purchased by a private individual. It has subsequently been determined to be the only copy known in public or private ownership and was offered for publication to the Devon & Cornwall Record Society. It is that map which has prompted this volume.

The map makes a significant contribution to the city's long history of map-making.

Seven Maps of Exeter

Richard Oliver & Roger Kain

Many people these days think of a 'town map' as synonymous with a 'street map': something to guide them as they move about the urban space, either on paper or as an 'app' in an electronic device. This was not the function of the maps reproduced in this volume. Most of them were published in or as appendages to books, or were otherwise too cumbersome to serve as useful guides on the ground. They were intended for display or for use in an office, library or study, or were consulted by 'armchair travellers' or students. Up to the middle of the nineteenth century maps could only be reproduced by relatively slow and expensive printing processes, and thus their circulation was restricted. At the same time most towns and cities were relatively compact: Exeter was one of the larger urban centres in Britain up to the later eighteenth century, yet the area within the walls measured only 788 metres from the east gate to the west, and 511 metres from the north gate to the south. One could easily walk the longer axis in less than a quarter of an hour. Development outside the walls took the form of ribbon-development along the main roads out of the city. The one place where a street map was definitely justified, on both logistical and commercial grounds, was London, which, then as now, was vastly bigger than any other British city, and for which from 1675 a steady stream of maps aimed at 'strangers' was published. The size of the city, its status and the consequent market made these ventures worthwhile. Even for Exeter, the fourth or fifth largest city in Britain in the sixteenth and seventeenth centuries, such 'strangers' mapping just was not justified. The idea that to have access to a street map when staying in a town, alongside a hotel reservation, is a development of the mid-nineteenth century onwards. Mass map-use is a relatively recent development. Even then, the 'map' as commonly understood is not necessarily the optimum form of wayfinding. The spread of satellite navigation systems since the early 1990s indicates that 'graphicacy' is not something that is 'natural' to many people: instructions to go forward, turn off, and so on save frequent looking at a map, or wrestling with an uncongenial tool.

Exeter's economic importance was one reason why it was mapped as an entity earlier and more often than most other urban areas in Britain, at any rate up to the early nineteenth century. The first published urban maps were of London and Norwich, produced near-simultaneously in the late 1550s. The London map was a massive thing, designed for wall-display by the prosperous; the Norwich map illustrated a manual of surveying, though it was not well integrated with its text. A map of Cambridge – once again, to illustrate a book – appeared in 1574; Oxford was provided with a wall-map in 1588.[1] Exeter joined what was still, in Britain, an elite few in 1587 with its map by John Hooker [Figure 1]. All these maps were copied, with varying degrees of fidelity, a number of times over the next century and more.[2] There was a good economic reason for this. Surveying was relatively expensive, and so more of a case had to be made for a new survey than for reusing an existing one. As maps were copied the information embodied in them was liable to degrade, and the interest of many of these copies today is less in the topography they profess to represent and more in the circumstances and methods of their production. The maps included in this volume are those where, because they are original surveys, the balance of interest lies towards the topography rather than the how and why they were made.

Of all the varied genres of mapping conducted in the sixteenth to nineteenth centuries, three in particular stand out as relevant to Exeter: topographic mapping, typically of whole counties, at relatively small scales; mapping of landed properties, at relatively large scales; and urban mapping, at a variety of scales.

I – John Hooker's map, 1587

Hooker and his map

John Hooker (1525–1601) is an example of 'the right man in the right place at the right time', and is perhaps Exeter's best candidate for status as a renaissance polymath.[3] He was educated both in England and, in the 1540s, at Strasbourg and Cologne; he subsequently studied law. In 1555 he was appointed the Exeter City's Chamberlain, which included responsibility

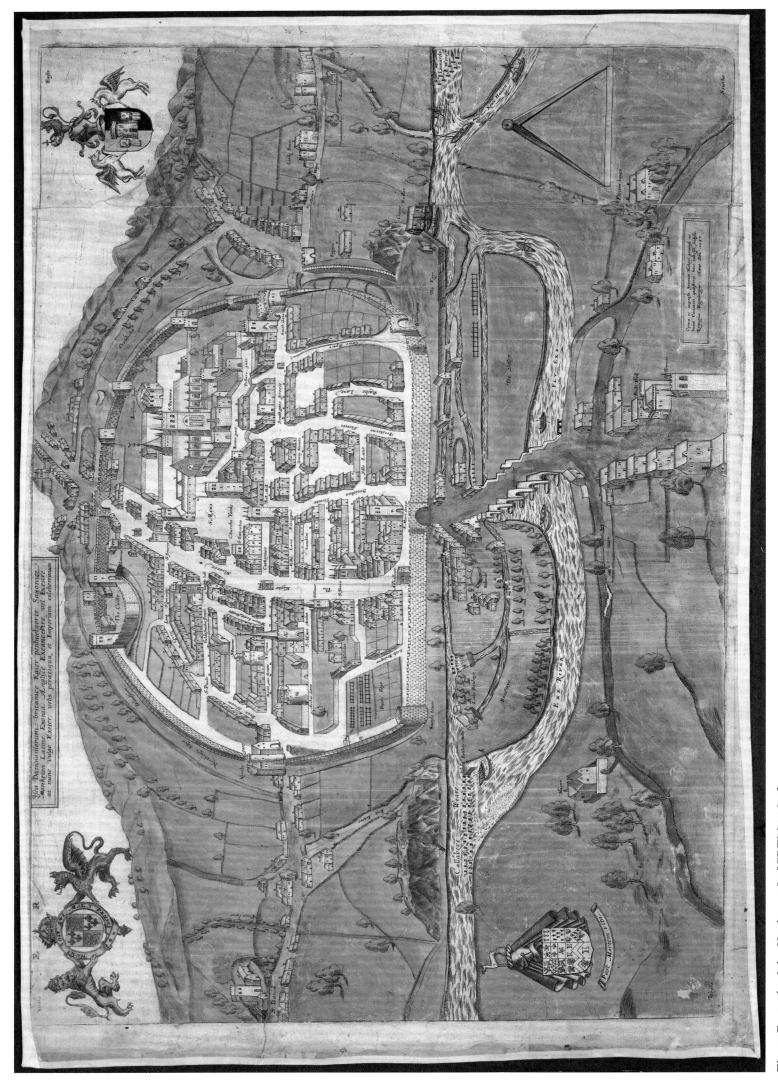

Fig. 1. Exeter by John Hooker, 1587 [CBTM 20603]

for the municipal records. Hooker went beyond this custodial function to collate the records of the city to produce a history of it in documents and extracts, which remained in manuscript until transcribed and edited in the twentieth century.[4] No doubt he found his *Description* of the city useful for effectively discharging his role of chamberlain: it must have appealed strongly to his sense of scholarship. His other work included continuing and editing Holinshed's *Chronicles*, which Shakespeare found so useful for his 'history' plays. His studies at Strasbourg may have included surveying, which was taught there: at any rate, he produced some small maps of parts of Exeter as aids to understanding leases. He gave a figure of 1600 paces of 5 feet for the circumference of the city, that is 8000 feet, which agrees quite well with the true figure of about 7700 feet (about 2350 metres). If anyone was likely to produce a map of Exeter then it was Hooker.[5]

Hooker's map of Exeter and his illustrative plans [Figure 1] embrace two of the divisions of domestic cartography, and he may have had contact with the third, topographical mapping, through Christopher Saxton. It has been plausibly suggested that, at some time before 1575, Saxton visited Devon to prepare a map of the county as part of his national survey of England and Wales and, while there, came into contact with Hooker; subsequently Hooker acquired a copy of Saxton's published map.[6] The Devon map was engraved by Remigius Hogenberg (*c*.1536–*c*.1588), a religious refugee from Antwerp, in what was then the Spanish Netherlands; he also engraved Hooker's map of Exeter. It is possible that, impressed with Hogenberg's work on the county map, Hooker was determined to have none other for his city map.

The plate for this map does not survive – very few such do – but it would have been a thin sheet of copper into which the design of the map was incised in reverse. Copies were obtained by rubbing ink into the engraved areas of the plate, and passing the plate, with a sheet of damped paper laid on it, through a roller press, in order that, as a much later writer put it, the ink transferred its affections from plate to paper. The plate was the penultimate document in the production of the finished map: it is probable that Hooker produced a much larger-scale manuscript original, which has not survived. The plate would have been capable of yielding several hundred copies before it showed signs of wear, which could be mitigated by touching up. The image of Hooker's map measured 51.2 by 35 centimetres; the plate would have been a little larger, to provide a 'handling edge'.

If the number of surviving copies is any guide, the Saxton atlas, published in 1579, was an Elizabethan best-seller. This cannot be said of Hooker's map: only three copies survive, yet each represents a different state of the plate. On the first there are dividers and a scale-bar, without graduations; on the second these have been deleted; and on the third a compass has been added. It has been suggested that the first version is a proof, and that the scale was deleted as unnecessary, for reasons to be discussed shortly. The third may date from after Hooker's death, or at any rate was produced without his connivance, as the map is oriented roughly north-east to south-west and north, east, south and west are indicated by text in the corners of the map, yet the compass disregards these.[7]

A map without a scale? What Hooker produced absolutely was a map, but one more in the nature of a bird's-eye view: an attempt to combine a plan of the city, showing the streets and principal buildings, with its appearance as viewed from the south-west, say from the top of Crossmead hill. At first sight Hooker's map looks eminently plausible: the high street, cathedral and castle are all where one expects to find them, and so is St Thomas's church in the foreground. However, the true ratio of the distance between the north and south gates and the east and west gates is about 1:1.53, whereas on Hooker's map it is about 1:0.65 – that is, the scale along the High Street axis is about half of that along North Street and South Street. Fidelity in apparent relative position is achieved by marked compression. William Ravenhill and Margery Rowe suggest that this was 'the application of perspective in an attempt to make a picturesque composition'.[8] The mean scale is about one inch to one hundred yards, or 1:3600, but the scale along the north–south axis is about 1:2400, whereas it is about 1:4800 along the west–east axis.

All buildings are shown pictorially; churches and other prominent buildings seem to be depicted with an attempt at realism; other buildings are shown in a stylised manner. There are limits to the realism: the cathedral is shown with apparently three bays to the west of the transeptal towers, and six bays to the east. Actually there are seven and eleven bays respectively. The north tower is shown with a pyramid roof or spire, which was removed in 1752–3. The bellcote of St Pancras is rather enlarged, and the towers of other churches appear somewhat stylised: St Thomas is depicted as a tower only. The river is enlivened by boats, but no-one walks the streets: to have shown the reality of people moving about would have confused the image. The walls are shown complete, with towers and gates.

Loyalty is expressed through the arms on the map: top left are the royal arms, top right are those of the city (with its quite recently acquired motto, 'Semper fidelis' – 'always faithful') and bottom left are Hooker's arms, with his motto 'Post mortem viva', and indeed this map's earthly service long outlived its maker's.

Hooker's motives for producing the map are unknown: his great compilation remained unpublished, and the map has not been associated with any published book. Had it been, probably more copies would have survived. Perhaps it was a 'vanity project', celebrating his native city. If so, it was perhaps more a success of local prestige than as a commercial proposition.

Hooker's numerous copiers

As was noted before, it is much easier to copy a map than to survey one afresh, and Hooker provided the material for at least seven imitators – or nine, if we include a version of his map that was painted onto a screen, and a manuscript derivative.[9] There were two groups of imitators: British and mainland European. The first copier was John Speed, who showed unusual honesty in admitting that he 'put his sickle into other men's corn' [Figure 2]. His main work was the *Theatre of the Empire of*

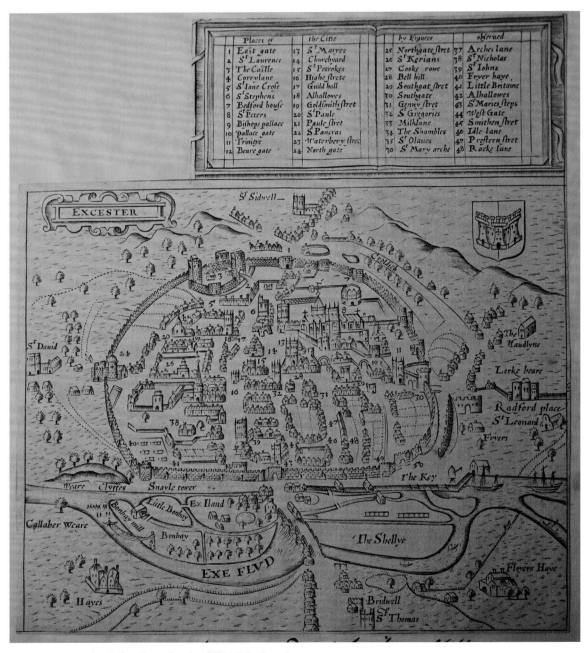

Fig. 2. Exeter by John Speed, 1611 [CBTM 18419]

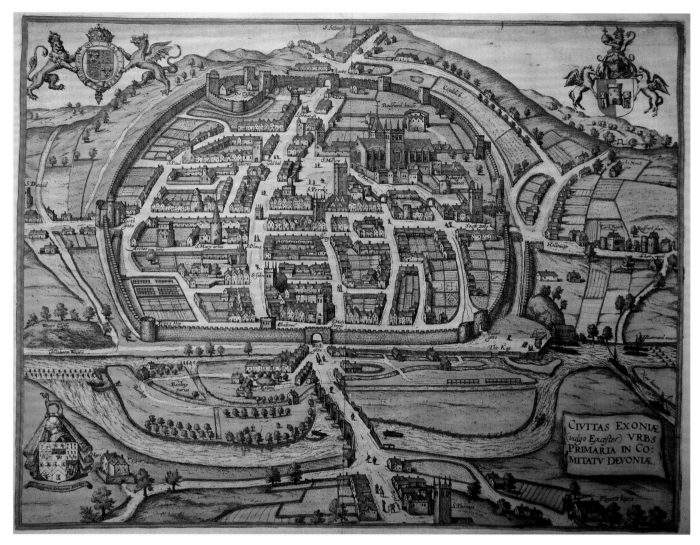

Fig. 3. Exeter by Braun & Hogenberg, 1618 [CBTM 18254]

Great Britain, an atlas of Britain that may have been inspired by the union of the English and Scottish crowns under James I/VI in 1603, though the main motive was probably financial.[10] His county maps were mostly copies of Saxton; they were supplemented by maps of county and cathedral towns. Although individual prints may have been sold, these were not maps suited to travellers for, in common with Saxton, they did not map roads. When, as at Exeter, there was an existing map, Speed cheerfully copied that, but he was only able to do that for about a dozen of the sixty-odd towns that he included: most of his urban maps derived from his own surveys.[11] While Hooker's map conferred prestige on Exeter, as being a city map in a land where there were as yet few such maps, in another sense Exeter did rather badly: had it waited for Speed, it would certainly have been mapped to a much higher standard of accuracy. Speed's copy was at a much smaller scale than Hooker's original, at a mean scale of 1:12,500: he reduced 'clutter' by replacing most of the text on the maps with numbers keyed to a reference-table. A peculiarity of this was that 48 numbers appear in the table, but numbers 21–23, 25, 33–37 and 41 do not appear on the map, whereas numbers 49 and 50 are written on the map but do not appear in the table. The extra numbers imply either that Speed visited the city and made some additions, or else that he had access to a written source, but failed to locate the buildings on the ground.

How did Speed come by a copy of Hooker's map? Did he encounter a copy in London? Did he visit Exeter, and ask if they were any maps or 'plats', and be shown a copy of Hooker's? We don't know.

What we do know is that Speed's atlas enjoyed a wider circulation than Saxton's, and that copies found their way to mainland Europe. The first imitator was in Georg Braun and Abraham Hogenberg's *Theatum Orbis Terrarum*, a six-volume compendium of plans and bird's-eye views of the cities of the world – or rather, those of which they were able to obtain plans to copy. Exeter was the first city to appear in the sixth and last volume, published in 1618[12] [Figure 3]. On the back of the map was a

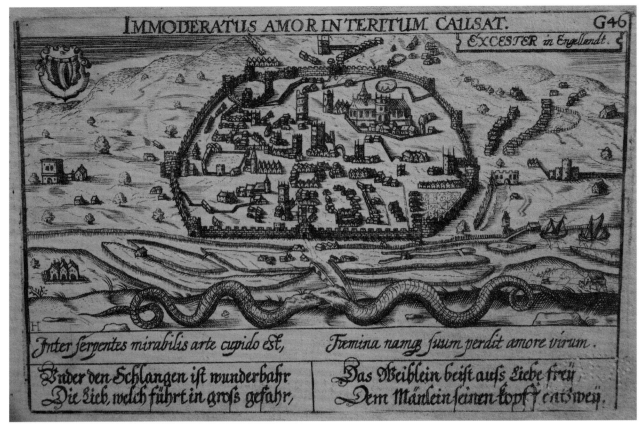

Fig. 4. Exeter by Daniel Meisner, 1631 [CBTM 18750]

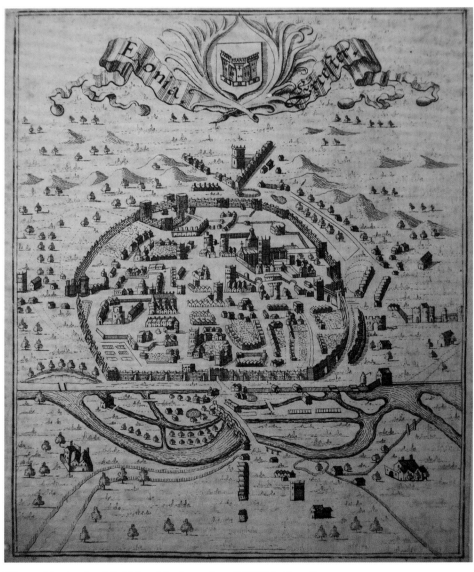

Fig. 5. Exeter by Matthias Merian, 1650 [CBTM 18302]

description of the city, which was printed in Latin, French and German versions. As with Saxton and Speed's offerings, *Theatum Orbis Terrarum* was a massive reference atlas, not something to be carried about. It belonged, in concept and use, to a 'virtual reality' world of scholarship, rather than of travel. It is indicative of this dichotomy that the map proper lacks text: in contrast to Hooker's unpeopled streets, Braun and Hogenberg have figures strolling about urbanely and conversing earnestly. The approach seems to have been generated as much by aesthetic as by graphical considerations: the lower part of Hooker's image was 'tidied up' by omitting the branch-channels of the River Exe, most of the industrial buildings, and all of St Thomas. It was a city without obvious geographical context. The plate, 40.3 by 31.8 cm, was reissued by Joann Jansson in 1660 in *Illustriorum principumque urbium septentrionalium Europae tabulae*.

Later imitators of Hooker, probably mediated via Speed or Braun and Hogenberg, were more interested in compactness than in detail. Daniel Meisner of Nuremburg included Exeter in the seventh volume of *Libellus novus politicus emblematicus civitatum*, first issued in 1631 and reissued in 1638 and 1700[13] [Figure 4]. This was a collection of town plans with emblems and morals: that for Exeter had a snake devouring another snake and a moral that translates as 'Excessive love causes death'. His map measures 14.3 by 9.8 cm: less than a third, in lineal dimensions, of Hooker's. In 1650 Matthias Merian of Frankfurt produced a similar-sized map, in a collection of seventeen town plans of Britain, which was reissued by J. C. Beer in 1690[14] [Figure 5]. Both Meisner's and Merian's maps lack geographical text and concentrate instead on the purely pictorial; this perhaps indicates derivation from Braun and Hogenberg rather than Speed. In 1661 Rutger Hermannides included Exeter in another volume of town plans, this time 13.0 by 10.5 cm; he named the river, but nothing else, and thereby suggested derivation from Speed rather than Braun and Hogenberg[15] [Figure 6].

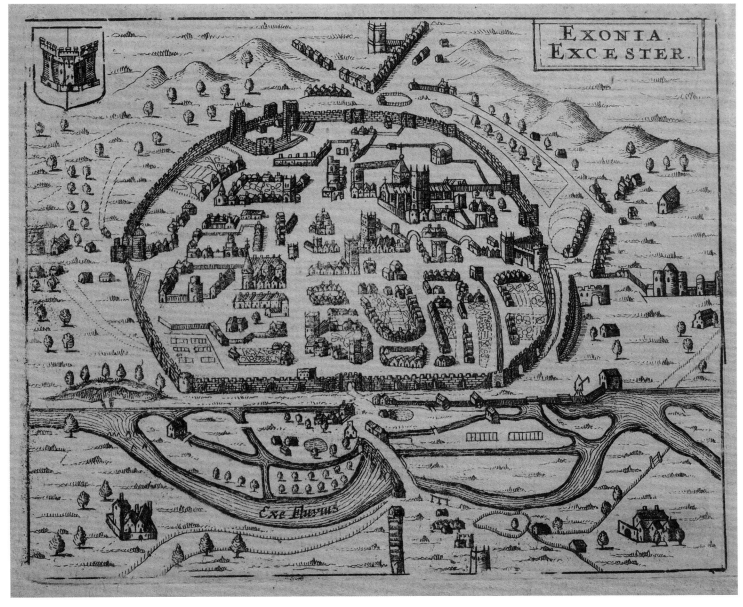

Fig. 6. Exeter by Rutger Hermannides, 1661 [CBTM 18749]

The first Englishman after Speed to copy Hooker's work was Richard Izacke: a map of Exeter, 21.5 by 16.2 cm, was included in *Antiquities of the City of Exeter, collected by Richard Izacke, Esquire*, published in 1677 [Figure 7]. Like Hooker, Izacke was Chamberlain of Exeter: he was less of a scholar than was Hooker, and the *Antiquities* was a less than perfect copying of Hooker's material, without due acknowledgement. While the map is Hooker's survey, its immediate derivation is from Speed: the copy retains Speed's numbering, and peculiarities.

The last of the known published copies of Speed was by Philip Lea, around 1689[16] [Figure 8]. Whereas Speed had reworked Saxton, Lea had acquired Saxton's plates, and squeezed town plans onto them. Exeter was less compressed than some: 13.0 by 11.3 cm was a modest reduction from Speed, though a considerable one from Hooker's engraving.

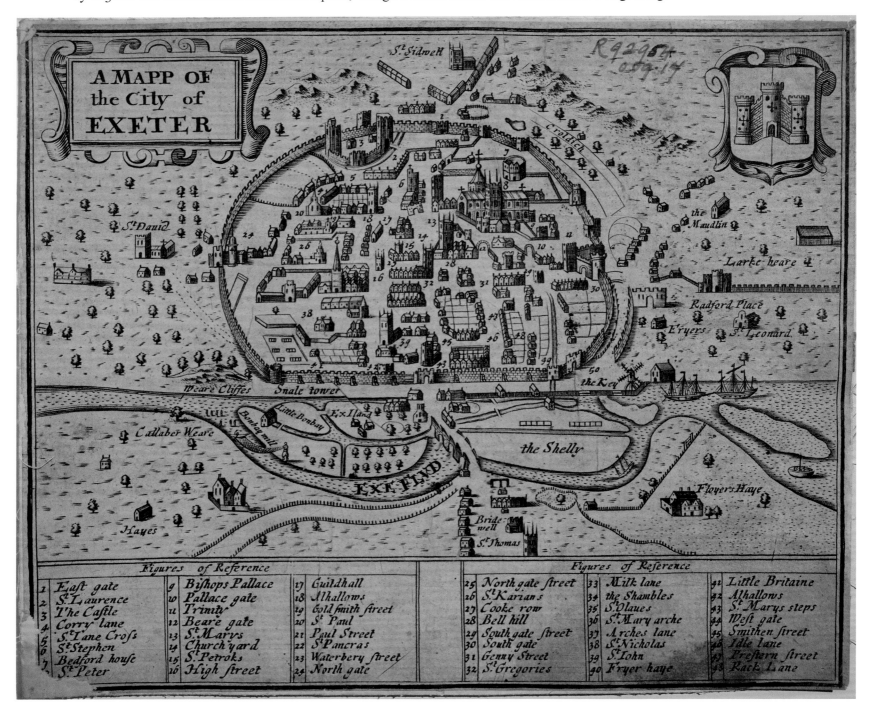

Fig. 7. Exeter by Richard Izacke, 1677 [CBTM 18307]

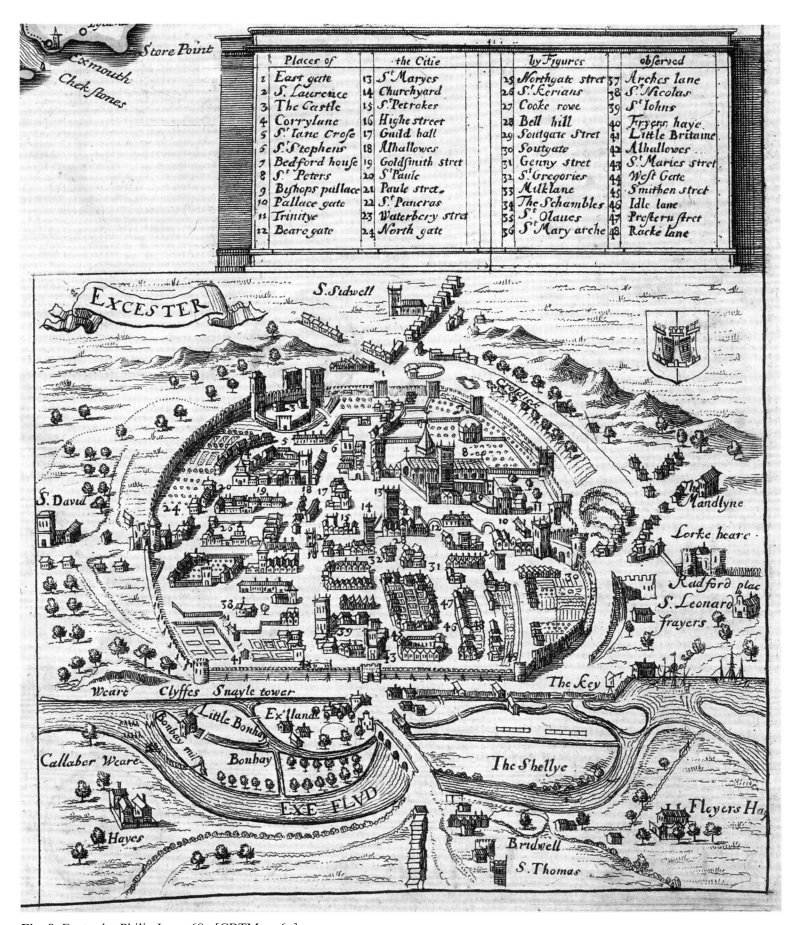

Places of		the Citie		by Figures		observed	
1	East gate	13	St Maryes	25	Northgate stret	37	Arches lane
2	S. Laurence	14	Churchyard	26	St Kerians	38	St Nicolas
3	The Castle	15	St Petrokes	27	Cooke rowe	39	St Iohns
4	Corrylane	16	Highe street	28	Bell hill	40	Fryers haye
5	St lane Crosse	17	Guild hall	29	Soutgate Stret	41	Little Britaine
6	St Stephens	18	Alhallowes	30	Soutgate	42	Alhallowes
7	Bedford house	19	Goldsmith stret	31	Genny stret	43	St Maries stret
8	St Peters	20	St Paule	32	St Gregories	44	West Gate
9	Bishops pallace	21	Paule stret	33	Milklane	45	Smithen stret
10	Pallace gate	22	St Pancras	34	The Schambles	46	Idle lane
11	Trinitye	23	Waterbery stret	35	St Olaues	47	Prestern stret
12	Beare gate	24	North gate	36	St Mary arche	48	Racke lane

Fig. 8. Exeter by Philip Lea, 1689 [CBTM 21160]

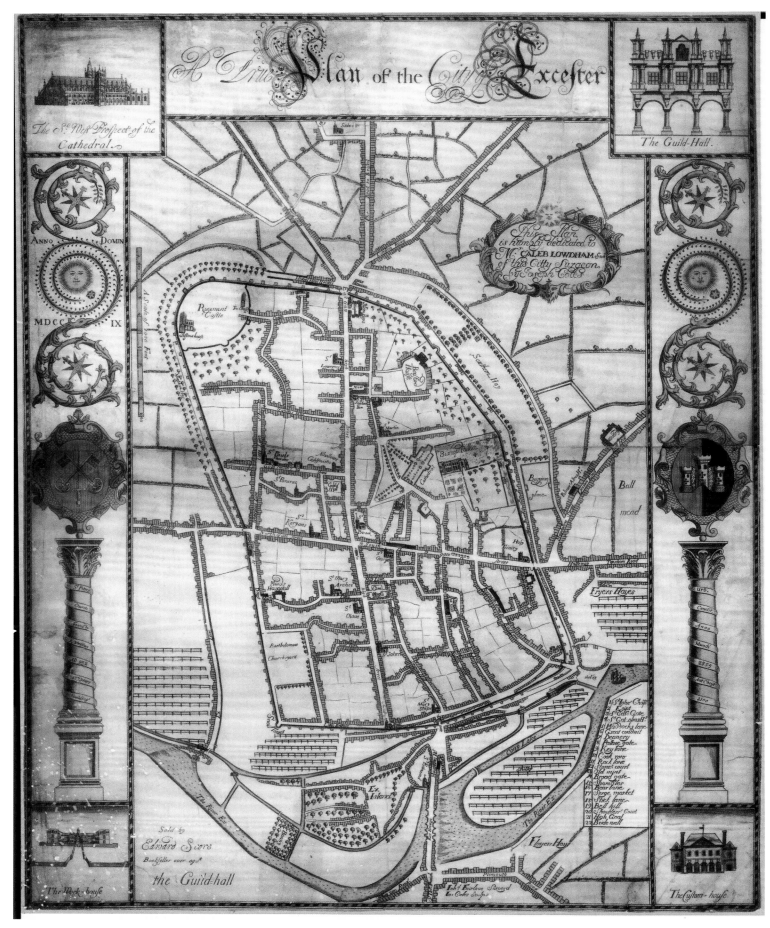

Fig. 9. Exeter by Ichabod Fairlove, 1709 [CBTM 18305]

II – The remapping of Exeter, 1709 [Figure 9]

In 1709 a new map of Exeter was published. It was surveyed by Ichabod Fairlove, engraved by Joseph Coles, goldsmith, dedicated to Caleb Lowdham of Exeter, surgeon, and sold by Edward Score, 'over against the Guildhall'.[17] Joseph Coles, the earliest recorded Exeter engraver, also engraved plates for the archaeological works of William Musgrave's *Iulii Vitalis epitaphium* published in 1711. It differed from Hooker's map in a number of respects. First, in common with Hooker but unlike his imitators, it appears to have been an independent production, rather than produced for a book or an atlas; it was a map that stood or fell on its own merits. Second, it was true to scale: from the scale-bar, which is placed a little awkwardly top left and may be an afterthought, this can be confirmed by comparison of the distances between the north and south and west and east gates, which are close to the true ratio of 1:1.53. The scale of the map is one inch to eighty yards: 1:2880. The alignment of the main street – now Fore Street and High Street – is relatively correct, with a bend west of the Guildhall. The general shape of the city within the walls is true, except for an excessive 'bulge' around the castle. This clearly implies that the map derives from a measured survey. The third difference is the treatment of buildings. Churches, the bishop's palace and the castle are shown pictorially, except for the cathedral, which is shown in plan, as are the remaining secular buildings. Otherwise, buildings are shown as 'ribbons' along streets, with schematic divisions to suggest plots. Every three divisions or so the back of the 'ribbon' is protruded. The walls are shown in plan; gates, whether standing or not, are indicated by gaps in the wall [Figure 10]. Most streets are named, either *in situ* on the map or via a numbered key. Only places of worship of the established church are named: the Toleration Act of 1689 had led to several dissenting sects quickly building their chapels – for example, the Quaker Meeting House east of Wynard's Hospital in 1692 – but there is no hint of this on the map. Dissent from the Anglican church might be tolerated, but there was seemingly no reason to acknowledge it by mapping it. The Quakers were a cartographic as well as a worshipping silence. The importance of the cloth industry to Exeter – a main reason for the city's prosperity, and indeed the economic rationale for producing a map such as this – is shown by the extensive depiction of tenter frames for drying cloth by the river. At the corners of the map were vignettes of the cathedral, the guildhall, the custom-house and the workhouse. Overall, it was rather larger than Hooker's map: 43 by 55 cm.

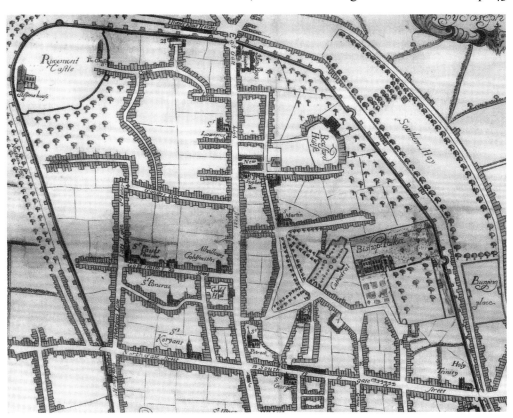

Fig. 10. Detail of walls & gates in Fairlove's map of Exeter, 1709

What were the motives in making this map? It is just possible that there was some unrecorded administrative function, but the dedication and the vignettes suggest that this was a commercial speculation, intended for wall-display: the vignettes seem celebratory rather than functional. Three original copies of the map are known in libraries: it can be conjectured that it was not a large seller outside the immediate vicinity.[18]

Fairlove's map was less prodigal in derivatives than was Hooker's. In 1723 Samuel Izacke produced a new edition of his father's plagiarising of Hooker, and duly included a half-scale – one inch to 160 yards, 1:5760 – version of Fairlove's map,

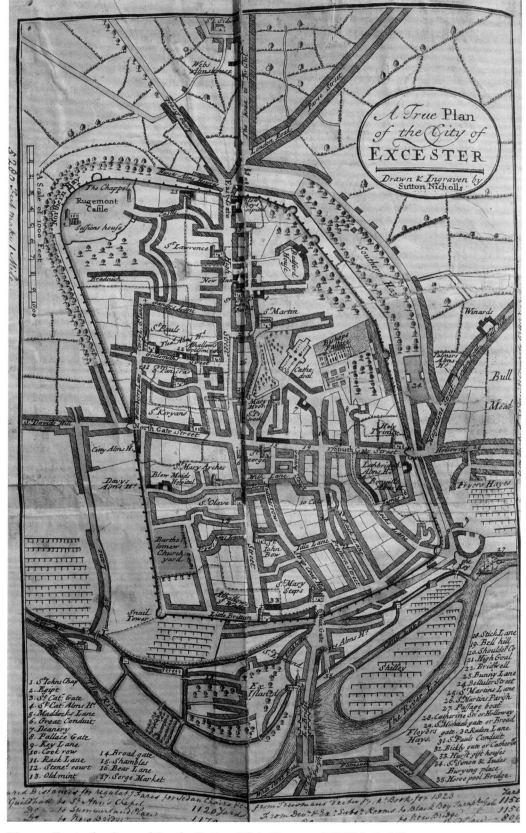

Fig. 11. Exeter by Samuel Izacke/Sutton Nicholls, 1723 [CBTM 18266]

measuring 16.8 by 25.7 cm and engraved by Sutton Nicholls[19] [Figure 11]. The overall effect was less refined; buildings along the streets were indicated by plain 'ribbons', without either schematic plot-divisions or rear protrusions. Nicholls followed Fairlove in indicating buildings and streets by a mixture of names *in situ* and a numbered reference.

In 1723 William Stukeley, the antiquary, visited Exeter and included a map of the city in his *Itinerarium Curiosum*, published the next year[20] [Figure 12]. Although he saw a copy of Hooker's map on the premises of Joseph Coles, his outline resembles Fairlove, with the rear protrusion of buildings characteristic of the original.[21] Stukeley does not name any streets within the walls, and he names fewer buildings than do Fairlove or Nicholls. The map is at a scale of one inch to 520 feet (1:6240) and measures 16.2 by 27.8 cm: conveniently page-sized. Though Constable in 1932 thought that Stukeley's was an independent production, idiosyncrasies of road patterns, notably outside the (unnamed) east gate, suggest copying and editing rather than wholly original survey.

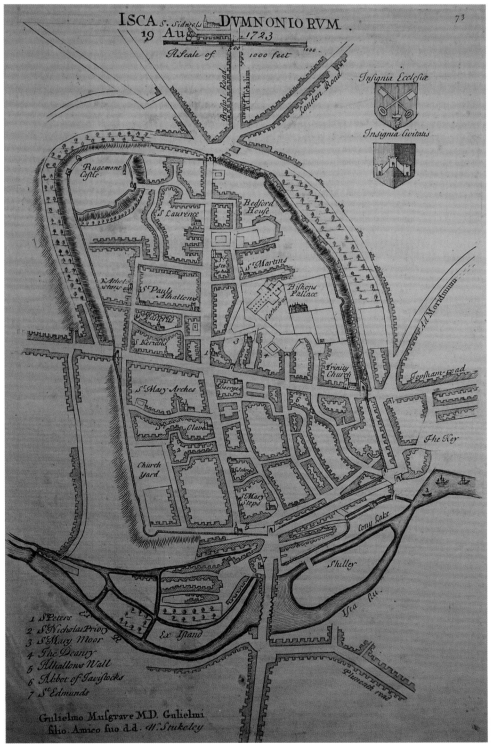

Fig. 12. Exeter by William Stukeley, 1723/24 [CBTM 18306]

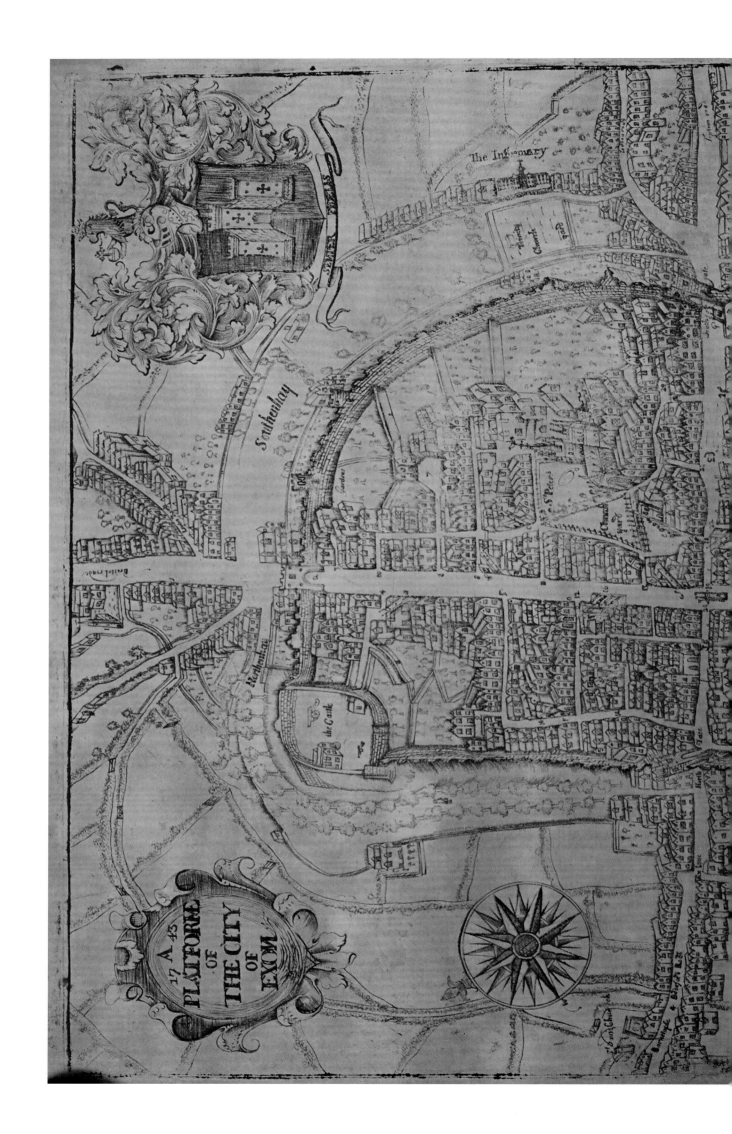

A 1743 PLATFORME OF THE CITY OF EXON

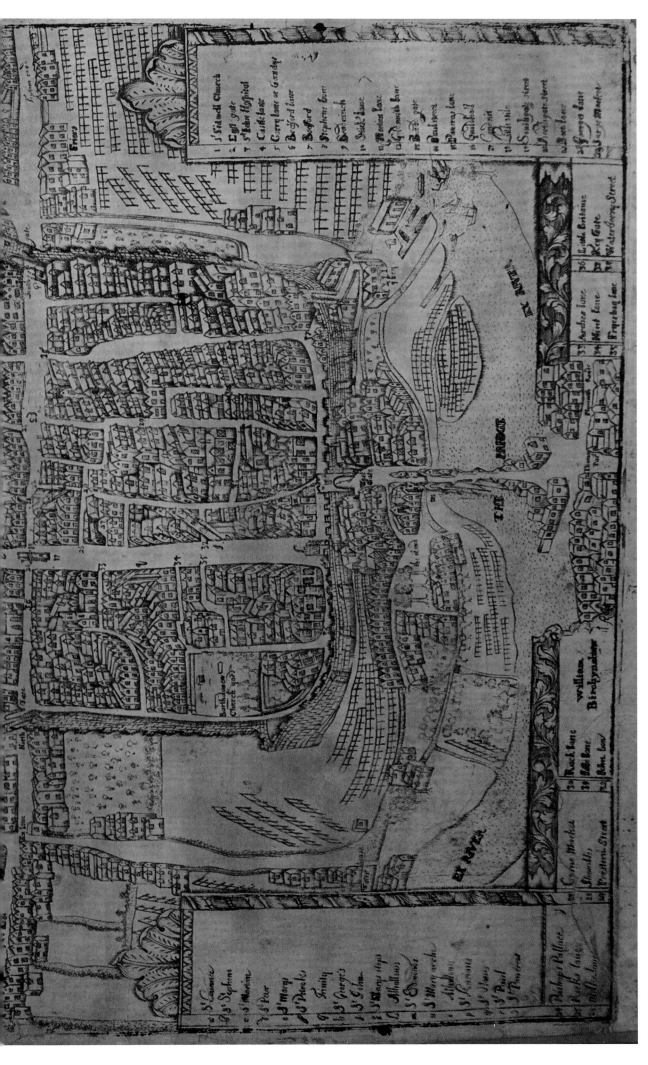

Fig. 13. Exeter by Birchynshaw, 1743 [*not in CBTM*]

III – The Birchynshaw map of 1743 [Figure 13]

Whereas Hooker's survey had enjoyed a currency of over 120 years, Fairlove's lasted only about a quarter of that time. Hitherto it has been assumed that it was replaced by Rocque's map of 1744, but a recent discovery has, at the least, called that assumption into question.[22] It is titled *A 1743 platforme of the city of Exeter*; the name 'William Birchynshaw' appears near the bottom of the map. The map has no indication of scale, but the ratio of distances between the north and south and west and east gates is 1:1.53, that is, similar to both Fairlove and to the true distance on the ground. A noticeable difference from Fairlove is that Fore Street, High Street and Sidwell Street run in practically a straight alignment, without the bends near the Guildhall and beyond the east gate. The city wall is without the noticeable 'bulge' by the castle shown by Fairlove and his derivatives, although on the south-east side there is a greater tendency to a smooth curve than there is on Fairlove, or is justified by reality. As on Fairlove, there is no indication of dissenters' places of worship. The map measures 32.1 by 38.3 cm, and comparative measurement suggests an intended scale of one inch to one hundred yards, or 1:3600: this is similar to the mean of Hooker's scales.

The map presents two big problems. The first is that it is not apparently a derivative of any previous known survey; either it has been surveyed independently, or it represents a heavily edited and modified version of a known survey – which effectively means Fairlove, as Hooker's map would not have provided Birchynshaw with the correct ratio of distances between the gates. The indications are contradictory: on the one hand the overall shape is 'accurate', but on the other hand details are not very accurate. The content of the map includes extensive pictorial tenters, which might derive from Fairlove, but it extends rather further than Fairlove does from the north gate into St David's, and there are differences in spelling of some names.

The second problem is the style of cartography, which is decidedly out of date for the 1740s. Everything is shown pictorially, in the way that it is on Hooker, but without Hooker's refinement. William Birchynshaw's status is uncertain, but whether he or another was the surveyor or cartographer, then the map's maker was seemingly not very skilled. Against this it must be admitted that the depiction of hedges and fields outside the city walls is quite delicate. The only William Birchynshaw who has been identified so far was a Freeman of Exeter who was recorded as a pewterer in 1723 and 1745: Birchynshaw is a local name.[23]

One answer might be that the date '1743' is an alteration or addition, and that the plate was first engraved much earlier. The date certainly looks as though it might have been inserted after the rest of the title cartouche had been laid out and incised, and a date of around the 1680s could be possible on the grounds of both style – if a little old-fashioned – and of the inclusion of the Custom House (built 1680–1). However, a simple reissue of an old plate appears to be ruled out by the inclusion of the 'Hospital' (the (Royal) Devon & Exeter) of 1742–3. The depiction of the hospital with a spire rather than a cupola may be an example of the mapmaker's tending to 'vertical exaggeration'. This trait is noticeable in the depiction of St Pancras church, where the bellcote becomes a full-blown spire, and at the cathedral, where the north tower is crowned with quite an elaborate spire.[24] These consistent vertical exaggerations suggest that the same hand was responsible for the depiction throughout – which is unlikely to be the case had a plate several decades old been updated. The engraving of the hospital appears to be somewhat darker than some of the other detail on the map [Figure 14]: this may indicate that it was a later addition – in which case a seventeenth-century origin is still possible – but it is noticeable that the engraving elsewhere is uneven, so the engraving of the hospital may not say much, other than that the map was thoroughly up to date in respect of public buildings for 1743. It may be that Birchynshaw drew the original map and that more than one engraver was responsible; alternatively, Birchynshaw could have engraved the map himself, and 'learnt on the job'. His work as a pewterer would presumably have included decorating and inscribing; the engraving of maps on copper had developed in the early sixteenth century from similar incising work by silversmiths. The somewhat fuzzy line of the engraving, less sharp than on a new copperplate, might suggest that it was engraved on a softer pewter plate, which would take a smaller number of impressions.

Why was the map made, and why has it remained unknown until now? The motives for its making may be similar to those of the Fairlove map: a commercial speculation, designed to appeal to local patriotism: the city arms appear top right. It may even have been for personal satisfaction. [*See above.*] The uneven and unrefined nature of the engraving would be unlikely to 'wow' many booksellers. Perhaps enhancement with hand-colour would have improved sales prospects? It is possible that the single surviving copy is either a proof, or possibly a much later print from a plate that may have survived into the twentieth

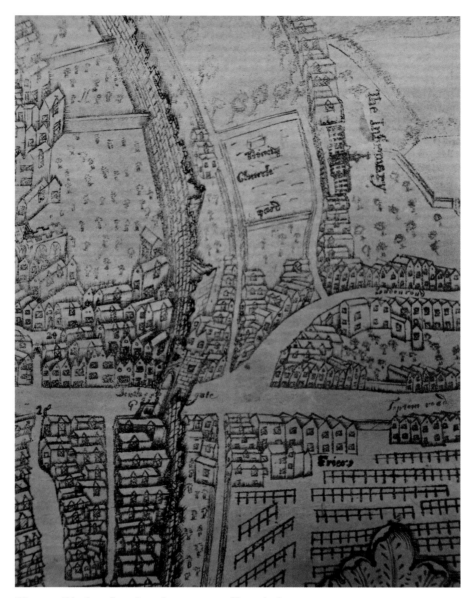

Fig. 14. Birchynshaw's enlargement of hospital, 1743

century, but then fallen victim to a scrap metal drive in one of the World Wars. Perhaps, and may be more likely, the venture may have been aborted when news of John Rocque's survey became known, later in 1743.

The provenance of the single surviving copy is uncertain: it is mounted on twentieth-century board, with '£7/10/=' on the back, which suggests that it was offered for sale in a shop some time before 1971. Otherwise the trail is cold.

IV – John Rocque, 1744 [Figure 15]

On 3 April 1743 Exeter City Council recorded:

Ordered that the Town C[ler]k do draw an advertisement in the nature of an encouragement to ye work intended by Mr Rocque for engraving a Plan of this City and deliver the same to him to be printed – taking for a [*illegible*] the encouragement given by ye City of London for the like work there.[25]

While not all the details of John Rocque's life and work have been elucidated, he is, compared with Birchynshaw, a well-known figure.[26] Rocque (c.1706?–61) was probably of French birth and certainly of Huguenot stock. His early career as

Fig. 15. Exeter by John Rocque, 1744 [CBTM 18290]

a surveyor entailed mapping parks and gardens; in 1737–45 he mapped London at a scale of one inch to 200 feet (1:2400), and then added the environs at a scale of one inch to 1000 feet (1:12,000); subsequently he published some smaller-scale maps of counties. He, therefore, straddled three genres of mapping: estate, urban and topographic. His maps included extensive decoration, both in the depiction of vegetation and in the titles and borders, and seemed aimed at display, portraiture and generating a sense of encyclopaedic knowledge in both the mapmaker and his customers. This was perhaps a façade, in more than one sense: his urban mapping is characterised by attention to streets and public buildings, but 'ordinary' buildings are indicated only by areas of stipple that conceal rather than reveal. A hierarchical society was in no danger from Rocque. His county maps, and maps of the environs of London, appear to be highly detailed, down to the level of showing hedges between fields, and the distinction of arable from pasture, but again this was a façade: impressionistic rather than exact.

As the London map drew near to completion and publication, Rocque needed another project. It is unclear how he came to light on Exeter, but evidently the fame of the London map was already enough in 1743 for Exeter to give Rocque the 'encouragement' that he sought. He got to work quickly: the map is dated 1744 and, if his dates are more reliable than some of the details of his cartography, it appeared before the map of London was completed.[27]

Like the London map it was large, being at the same scale of 1:2400, and aimed at display rather than convenience of use, never mind portability on the ground.[28] The map measured some 120 by 76 cm, and was divided between two copper plates. Despite its relative size, it seems to have sold in a way that Hooker and Fairlove had not, if surviving copies are any guide. Perhaps Rocque's push and professionalism persuaded Birchynshaw to abandon his more modest and distinctly less stylish project.

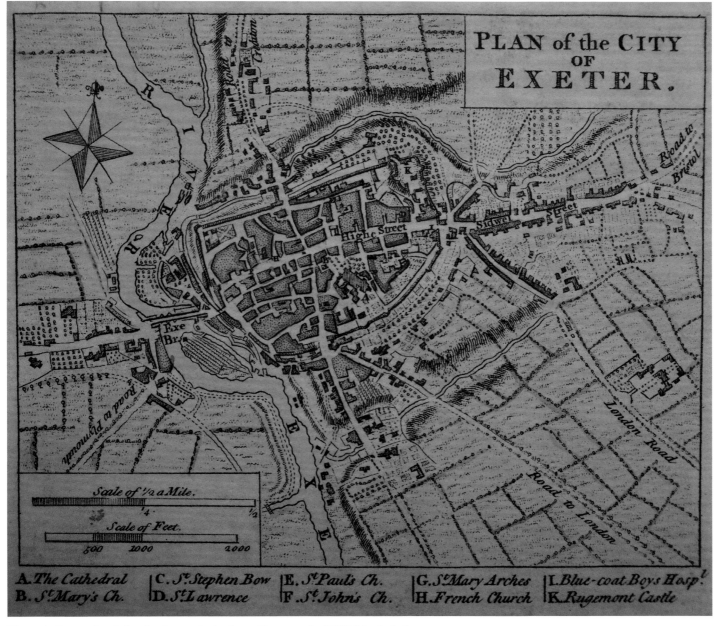

Fig. 16. Exeter by John Andrews & Andrew Dury, 1764 [CBTM 18389]

Rocque's mapping of Exeter was very similar to that of his London map: though the stipple of areas behind frontages evaded details, it at least avoided the stylised depiction of all previous maps of Exeter. Churches and important buildings are indicated by their 'footprints', including the cathedral. The unbuilt-on areas demonstrated Rocque's fondness for depicting land-cover: thus tenters appeared in profusion in the vicinity of the Exe. Elaborate ornament suggested extra-mural gardens. The city was hugged by the countryside. 'Clutter' was reduced by identifying many buildings by numbers, keyed to a reference. Rocque did not manage to outdo Fairlove or Birchynshaw in absolute accuracy: the north–south to east–west ratio was 1:1.58. The size and shape of the city were such that, rather than map the more outlying areas that could have been fitted into the map frame, Rocque provided nine illustrations, including a scene at Trew's Weir with naked male bathers, all in rococo framing. A sense of civic belonging was given by including not only the arms of the city and the diocese, but also those of the thirteen city trade companies. The effect for contemporaries was of an up-to-date portrait, and cosmopolitan sophistication: as was Rocque's practice, the title was in both English and French.

Rocque died in 1761; in 1764 his widow, Mary Ann, published a new version of the survey in a more manageable form, at half the scale (1:4800), and measuring 48.5 by 30.2 cm.[29] She milked to the full her husband's having been 'Topographer to His Majesty'.

Rocque's mapping was the basis for several derivatives. One, a small-format atlas of town plans, was published by Andrews and Dury in 1764[30] [Figure 16]. What appears to be a reworking of Rocque was the plan of Exeter that Benjamin Donn included as an inset on his one-inch scale county map of Devon of 1765[31] [Figure 17]. In its details this bears a close resemblance to Rocque. William Ravenhill suggested that the similarities were attributable to the two maps being only twenty years apart, but the general shapes of streets and such buildings as are mapped are very close: Donn follows Rocque in showing most buildings as generalised areas of stipple.[32] Particularly telling is the treatment of an area on the east side of the city where Rocque has illustrative matter: Donn only shows grassy ornament. Donn may have revised Rocque, but he does not appear to have replaced him.

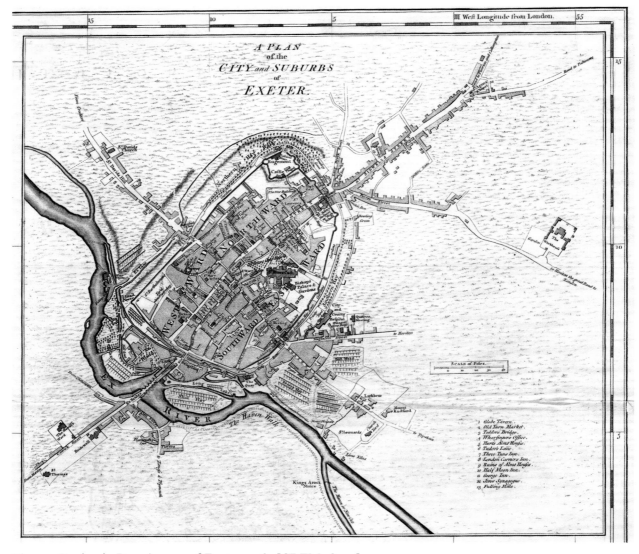

Fig. 17. Benjamin Donn's map of Exeter, 1765 [CBTM 18242]

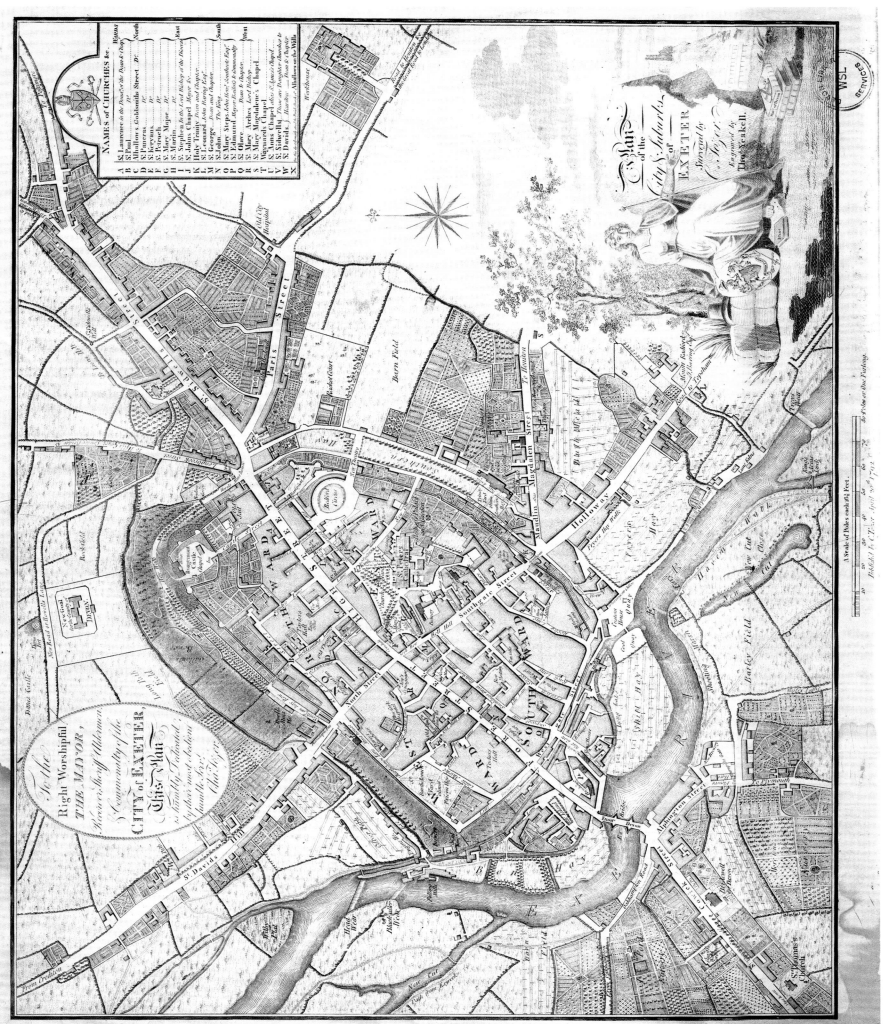

Fig. 18. Exeter by Charles Tozer, 1792 [CBTM 18255]

V – Charles Tozer, 1792 [Figure 18]

A fresh survey of Exeter was made by Charles Tozer and published in 1792.[33] It was dedicated to the (unnamed) Mayor and Corporation. The general style resembles Rocque, and it is unclear whether this was in fact a completely new survey, or whether Tozer used Rocque as a starting-point and subjected him to thorough revision. What is certain is that the map is much smaller than Rocque's: it is at a scale of one inch to six chains, 1:4752, and measures 40.8 by 34.3 cm. The style of building depiction is that of Rocque and Donn: buildings within the walls are indicated by areas of stipple; only churches and public buildings are mapped according to their shape. Like Rocque, Tozer shows unbuilt land with details of cultivation. The map was engraved by Thomas Yeakell, who otherwise seems to be known as a draughtsman for the Board of Ordnance.[34] The plate was still extant in 1977, when a number of copies were struck.[35]

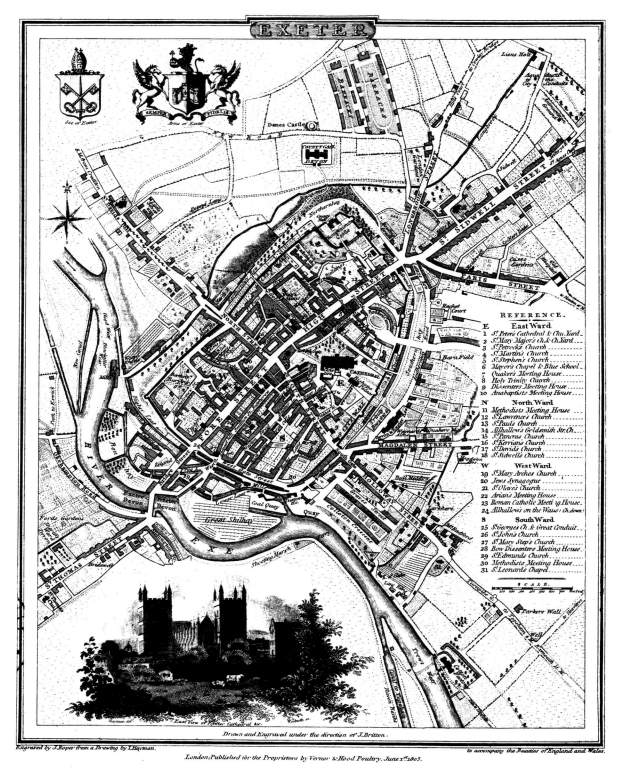

Fig. 19. Exeter by I. Hayman/John Britton, 1805 [CBTM 18256]

The motives for the production of Tozer's map are unknown. As with Fairlove's, it may have been a commercial venture. Tozer's map is likely to have been the starting-point for two maps of Exeter produced by J. Hayman, in 1805 and 1806. Both were published in books. That of 1805 appeared initially in the Devon section of John Britton's serialised *The beauties of England and Wales*, and in 1810 was included in *The British Atlas*, issued by William Faden, 'Geographer to the King'[36] [Figure 19]. *The beauties* was essentially a glamorous reference work, intended to appeal to a bourgeois antiquarian taste, and the choice of cathedral city maps seems to have been determined in part by what was available. The maps were decorated with city and diocesan arms, and suitable vignettes: that of Exeter featured the cathedral. The other map drawn by Hayman was included in Alexander Jenkins's history of Exeter, and had a much more limited circulation.[37]

Either one of Hayman's drawings or possibly Tozer's map probably served as the model for Brown's map of the city, published in 1835[38] [Figure 20]. It included recent building developments, which would have had to be surveyed by some means: this may have been by pacing and interpolation. The map includes four vignettes at the corners, and the diocesan and city arms: the moderately decorative border and the small scale – one inch to 240 yards, 1:8640 – and size – 25.2 by 19.9 cm – suggest that it was intended as much for hanging on a wall as for carrying about. Letters and numbers on the map were keyed to a reference, which included statistics for the number of houses in each parish; this data was no doubt taken from the 1831 census returns.

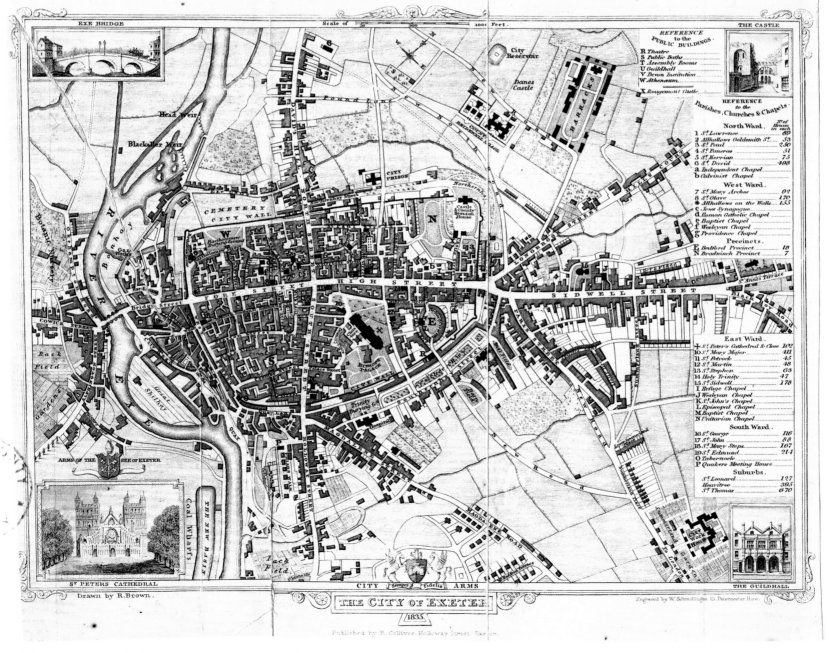

Fig 20. Exeter by R. Brown, 1835 [CBTM 18239]

VI – John Wood [Figure 21]

John Wood (*c*.1780–1847) was a Yorkshireman by birth, who has the distinction of having mapped more British cities and towns – at least 149 – than any other individual. His career and maps have been described by Brian Robson, and need only be summarised here.[39] Between 1818 and 1826 he made 53 maps of Scottish towns and cities: all but three he surveyed himself. Most of them were gathered together in an atlas, which was published in 1828. While this was a bulky reference volume, unsuited to the traveller, the maps were also available individually. The apparently comprehensive listing of inns on many of them suggests that one market was landlords, for wall-display as a service to their customers: a routine service, perhaps, which seems largely to have escaped notice, then and since.[40]

Well before the Scottish series was complete, Wood turned his attention to northern England. Whereas in Scotland he seems to have aimed at comprehensive national cover, in England, and later Wales, his maps fall into regional groups: he apparently made no maps at all in eastern or south-eastern England. He operated from a temporary office in a town, and used it as a base for mapping other towns in the vicinity. Thus he mapped Exeter, and then Taunton and Tiverton, followed by other towns in Devon. He mapped some towns in Dorset but apparently did not map any in Cornwall. Although the number of town maps suggests that his 'business model' was viable, many of his maps are only known from a single surviving copy, and more may yet be found.[41]

Wood's map of Exeter is dated 1840 and is at one inch to four chains (1:3168). It was relatively large: 81.2 by 67.8 cm. It is not one of his more detailed: buildings tend to be generalised, and there is no list of inns. However, various industries are shown around the quay and elsewhere, including brick works – necessary for the city's renewal and expansion – and 'White Lead', that is, paint. Overall, it remains the most detailed record of the early Victorian city.

Several maps of the city were produced after 1840: some may have been sold separately, to function as 'street maps' for visitors, and others were included in directories or guide books. The map of 1849 stated to have been 'corrected to the present time' by J. Warren and published by Henry Besley at the 'Directory Office' in South Street, was suited to both guide and directory use[42] [Figure 22 on page 28]. The basic map was probably derived from Wood: Warren added extensive recent suburban growth that was tending to fuse Exeter with Heavitree. While the urban part of St Thomas, as far west as the church, had appeared on Exeter city maps more often than not as far back as Hooker, and the same applied to St Sidwells in the opposite direction, Heavitree remained a place apart. St Thomas was administratively separate from the city up to 1900, latterly with formal 'urban' status; Heavitree, also latterly 'urban', remained separate until 1913, although the meanderings of the parish boundary meant that in practice some of the villas and semi-detached houses on the west side of the parish, and to the east of where the Diocesan Training College (now the St Lukes component of the University) was built in 1852, appeared on Exeter city maps.

An interesting feature of the Besley–Warren map is at the station (now St Davids): one access road is annotated 'From the train' and the other 'To the Luggage Train': unusual references to early railway practice. The continuation in the 1840s of what was later the main line of the Great Western Railway provided a convenient limit for the detail on the west side of a city map. This was duly done by John Tallis in his map of 1851[43] [Figure 23 on page 29]. This was part of a reference atlas, and included six vignettes round the edge: one of those was where otherwise St Thomas might have been mapped. Tallis's map may be derived from Besley's, with some generalisation and additions: it was much cheaper to send an artist who could sketch the vignettes and walk round the suburbs and sketch in new buildings – particularly in the prosperous and growing area of St Leonards – than to commission a completely new survey. The same principle applies to the various guide book maps of the second half of the nineteenth century. The precise means used to provide updated data is unknown – local correspondents is one possibility – but the results could sometimes be odd. The map in Murray's *Handbook* of 1863 shows the railway from Salisbury, opened in 1860, apparently entering from the north, through the hilly district of Pennsylvania, without the assistance of a tunnel[44] [Figure 24 on page 30].

Fig. 21. Exeter by John Wood, 1839 [CBTM 18312]

Fig. 22. Exeter by J. Warren/Henry Besley, 1850 [CBTM 1873]

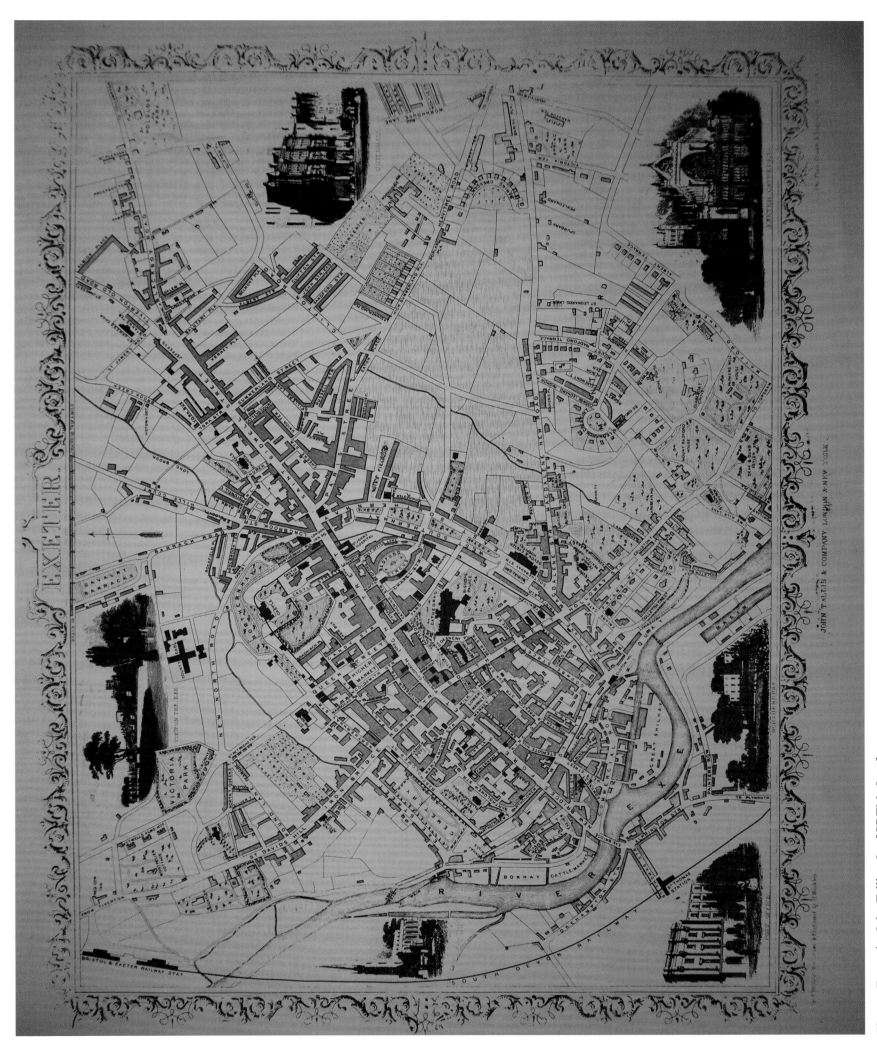

Fig. 23. Exeter by John Tallis, 1851 [CBTM 18257]

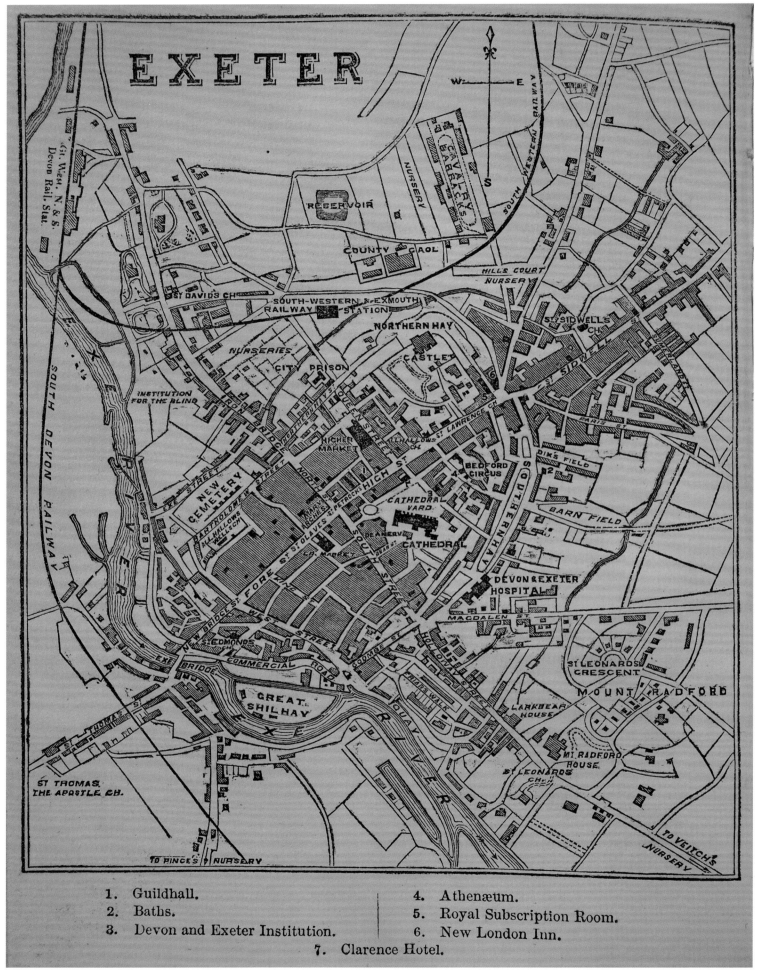

1. Guildhall.
2. Baths.
3. Devon and Exeter Institution.
4. Athenæum.
5. Royal Subscription Room.
6. New London Inn.
7. Clarence Hotel.

Fig. 24. Exeter in Murray's *Handbook for travellers in Devon and Cornwall*, 1863 [CBTM 18740]

VII – The Ordnance Survey [Figure 25]

The Ordnance Survey originated in the late eighteenth century mainly to produce mapping for military use: civil mapping was at first a sideline. The first published Ordnance mapping of Exeter was at the one-inch scale and went on sale in 1810. After 1815 the Survey developed entirely for civil purposes, and from the mid-1850s the standard scales of survey were 1:2500 for cultivated rural areas and 1:500 for towns of over 4000 population. From these, derived maps at the six-inch (1:10,560) and one-inch scales were produced. This mapping was both of unprecedented detail in content and decidedly protracted in the making. One way that towns could expedite the process, and be satisfied sooner than they would otherwise be, was by paying two-thirds of the cost of a 1:500 survey. Comparatively few towns did this, but Exeter was one such.[45] By 1874 there was concern as to what surveys of the city were available: this was probably in order that utility projects and infrastructure could be planned and recorded. Robert Dymond and Sons, a well-established local firm of land surveyors, was asked to report: they themselves owned a four-chain map of the city and county (this may have derived from John Wood's work), but reported that they considered that the city should be mapped at a scale of around one inch to forty feet (1:480): every important town already had such a plan, and 'our city is peculiar in being without one'. This was probably not entirely true, though it certainly was of Torquay, Brixham and Plymouth, but it was no doubt effective. Dymond cited the Torquay plan, and suggested an application to the Ordnance Survey. 'The Dymond letter proved to be an effective blend of technical argument with a telling appeal to civic pride.'[46] The adjoining parishes of St Thomas, St Leonard and Heavitree were apparently not interested in being included in the project, and so only those portions of those parishes necessary to fill up the Exeter sheets were surveyed. The survey, at 1:500, close to Dymond's suggested scale, was put in hand some time after October 1874, and the maps were published in 1876–7, both at 1:500 and at 1:2500. As they were produced in anticipation of the eventual mapping of the whole of Devon, they were laid out and numbered as part of Devon-wide sheet lines.

> The plans were produced by methods which ensured a high level of planimetric accuracy, and as well as the layout of all streets, lanes, alleys and courts, they show individual buildings and open spaces such as gardens down to the level of single trees, greenhouses, paths, statues and sundials. Indeed, the scale is large enough to show doorsteps and the thickness of walls. Numerous features are named, ranging from antiquities to industrial premises, while for public buildings – schools, prisons and workhouses – ground-floor layouts with an indication of the use of individual rooms is a notable feature of the plans. Both parish and ward boundaries are included…[47]

The maps were soon in use in the city to record sewers and water mains.[48] The rural areas adjoining Exeter – including St Thomas and Heavitree – were mapped at 1:2500 in 1887–8. As part of this process the 1:500 and 1:2500 mapping of Exeter of 1874–7 was fully revised, redrawn and republished, and the data was also used for less detailed mapping at the six-inch scale.

The Ordnance Survey provided a basic survey that could be, and was, drawn on as a standard source of spatial data. Although the 1:500 scale proved to be uneconomic to maintain, and the Exeter mapping at this scale was not updated after 1888, the smaller scales were continued, and indeed were joined by a 1:1250 scale after 1945. Indeed, because of war damage, and the opportunity for replanning, Exeter was one of the first cities mapped at the 1:1250 scale. That said, for many purposes the Survey's products were not completely satisfactory: they were produced on sheet lines that often cut across urban centres (Exeter was more fortunate than most in this regard), and much of the detail, such as administrative boundaries, was of interest only to specialist users. To use a fairly recent phrase, they seemed 'over-engineered'. Therefore the production continued of derived maps to suit a wider audience, particularly in regard to urban mapping. This led to the extensive production of a type of map sometimes seen in the nineteenth century, but ubiquitous for much of the twentieth, which concentrated on streets and buildings and spaces of public interest, but little else. Although colour-printing was readily available by the late nineteenth century, such street maps were usually monochrome, in order to keep the price down, though they might include extra colour on the cover. They were often produced on behalf of municipalities: thus by the late 1940s the Exeter Official Publicity and Information Bureau was issuing a map of the city at the four-inch (1:15,840) scale enlivened by bus routes being shown in green [Figure 26]. The municipal, secular character of the map was emphasised by the only urban church shown being the cathedral, though it also indicated the Corporation Transport Depot, swept away not long after by the Paris Street roundabout. On the reverse was advertising, and a cover panel printed in red, in which the city arms, with supporters,

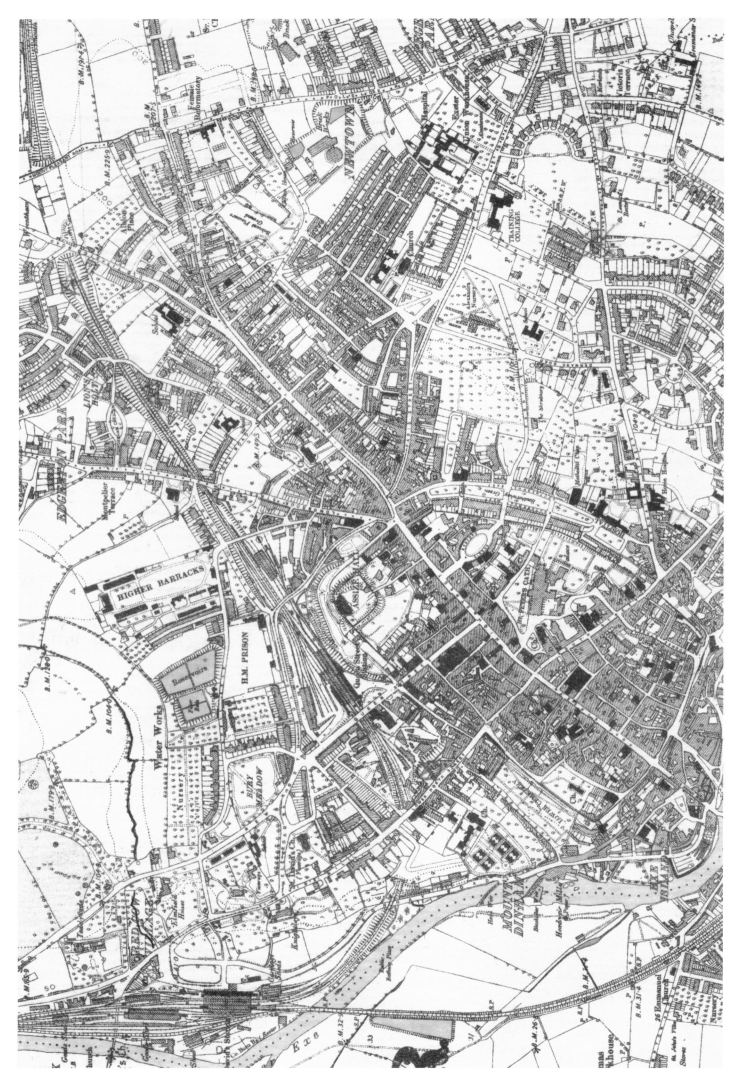

Fig. 25. Exeter, mapped by the Ordnance Survey in 1888: scale of original six inches to one mile [*not in CBTM*]

were a little incongruous above modern-looking Gill Sans typography. This mapping, redrawn in due course at the six-inch scale, was republished at frequent intervals, updated to show the expansion of both the residential and commercial areas: the latest version, first produced in the mid-1980s, with 'All recent developments included', at 1:11,792, is colour-printed. Technically and in looks it is a long way from Hooker, and one looks in vain for the city arms (they disappeared in the early 1970s), but it is produced by a local firm, Quail Maps, and includes bus routes and other details not to be found on Ordnance Survey mapping. Here is continuity: Hooker worked in a society conditioned by the need to prove loyal to the Elizabethan Settlement; the map of Exeter of over four hundred years later is conditioned by Ordnance Survey data.

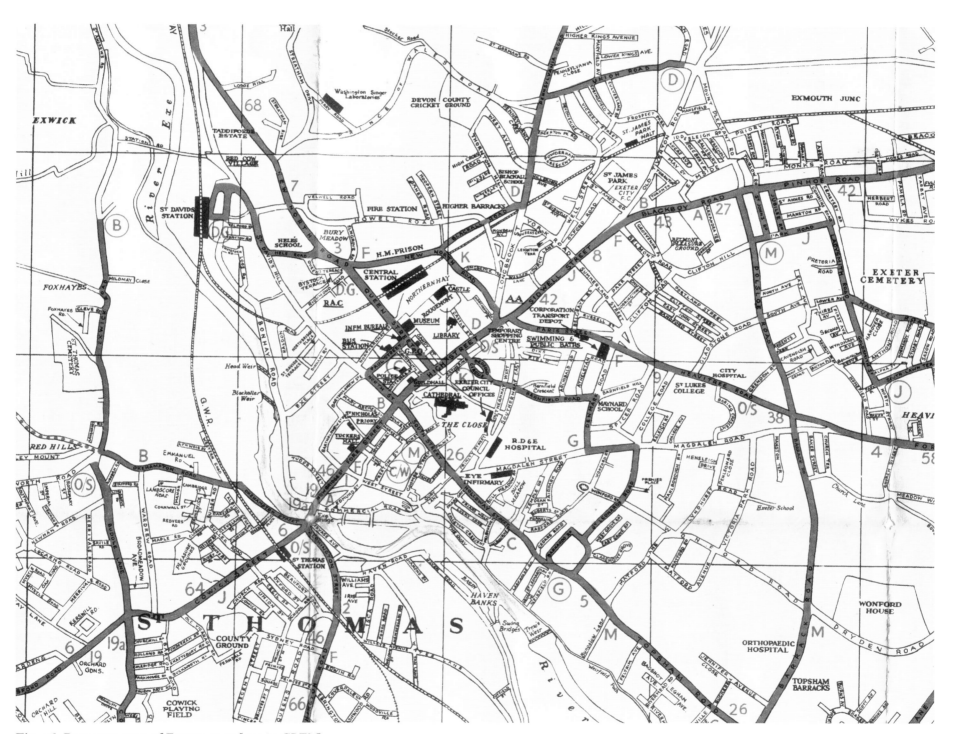

Fig. 26. Bus-route map of Exeter, 1949 [*not in CBTM*].

Exeter in 1743

Todd Gray

Early eighteenth-century visitors were invariably impressed by Exeter. They found Devon's capital exceedingly prosperous, filled with fashionable buildings and situated so as to provide fine prospects of the Exe Estuary. Had they read one guidebook of 1712 they would have anticipated seeing 'a large, compact and well-inhabited city', while a generation later others would have read of 'a fair and rich city' or 'a very large well-built city'.[49] However, at the close of the eighteenth century Exeter was viewed very differently: its cloth industry had all but disappeared, the townscape was increasingly criticised for its old-fashioned buildings and the streets were considered dirty and unwholesome. Nonetheless, in 1743, Exeter was still being acclaimed, though Exonians themselves were aware of a gradual waning and decline. In that same year, William Birchynshaw drew his map of Exeter, with which we are concerned here.

Topography

In 1743 all visitors travelling on the main road from Plymouth needed to pass through Exeter in order to reach their destinations. Devon's other southern roads also converged on Exeter because of its position on the tidal point of the river. The city was thus familiar to thousands of strangers.

Visitors were initially confronted with the high plum-coloured ancient stone wall, which stretched around Exeter for nearly two miles. After passing through one of the five gates, they discovered a street layout that had remained largely intact for centuries. Exeter had four, in reality two, main streets (High and Fore, North and South), which met at the Carfax, the crossroads. Near this junction stood the Great Conduit, and below the city the river was crossed only by the multi-arched medieval bridge. Birchynshaw drew all these features including the houses that were built on the sides of Exe Bridge following the Civil War. The city would not begin its 'Age of Improvement' for another two decades: it was not until the 1760s that the first gate was demolished, a bank was built and one of England's earliest hotels was opened.

Birchynshaw showed how the city's skyline was decorated with the short towers of sixteen parish churches inside the walls (Allhallows Goldsmith Street, Allhallows on the Walls, Holy Trinity, St George, St John, St Kerrian, St Lawrence, St Martin, St Mary Arches, St Mary Major, St Mary Steps, St Olave, St Pancras, St Paul, St Petrock and St Stephen) and another five outside (St Edmund, St David, St Thomas, St Sidwell and St Leonard). In 1700 an East Anglian visitor commented upon their size. They were: 'all so monstrously small that he that vaults well may either leap on or over the biggest of them without danger of breaking his limbs'.[50] Interestingly, Birchynshaw wrongly placed Holy Trinity Church on the western side of South Street.

Birchynshaw drew considerable detail including gardens behind Bedford House or possibly those of St John's Hospital at the top of High Street. He also attempted to capture Devon hedges; these appear as solid boundary walls with plants, sometimes trees, growing on the tops. What may have been orchards appear inside the city walls across from Southernhay, in the castle ditch and outside the North, East and West Gates.

Birchynshaw's trees may have been elms, which were known to have been the most conspicuous tree in and around Exeter, particularly in the promenade at Northernhay. In 1700 a traveller described its attractions. It was:

> a walk set with large elms on both sides, at least half a mile long, and public for all sorts and sizes of people, wonderfully pleasant and wonderfully clean being gravelled, which is so hard with continual tramping that it needs no rolling and goes by the name of Northernhay Walk, it encompasses the Castle on one side.[51]

The great storm of 1703 had felled other prominent elm trees in the cathedral precinct, which was generally known as St Peter's Churchyard before more recently being designated as either Cathedral Close or Cathedral Yard. Lime trees had been planted in their stead but were afterwards replaced by other elms, which were cut to resemble fans. The walkways around them were called the Exchange and had been in existence since at least the 1660s. In about 1746 it was noted: 'Here, as on a sort of Change, almost daily do gentlemen, merchants and chief traders walking take the Meridian Air and talk of business or of news perhaps or laugh at merry tales.'[52] By 1711 one of the coffee houses in St Peter's Churchyard was called The Exchange.[53]

Six of the most notable buildings were drawn and identified by Birchynshaw. Four of these can be easily seen: the cathedral, Rougemont Castle, the guildhall and the custom house. St Peter's Cathedral was constructed from the mid-eleventh century until the early fifteenth, and in 1743 still retained its wooden steeple, along with the cockerel weather vane, on the North Tower. Less than a decade later it was taken down.[54] Five of the thirteenth-century gates (Bear, Broad, Little Stile, Palace and St Catherine) around the cathedral precinct were drawn by Birchynshaw. Martin's Gate was omitted. Rougemont Castle, erected shortly after the Norman Conquest, has its Sally Port depicted. One visitor in 1724 commented: 'the walls are in pretty good repair, having many lunettes and towers'.[55] Birchynshaw drew two buildings within the castle wall which were seen by that same observer:

> in the northern angle of the city, and highest ground, is Rougemont Castle, once the royal residence of the West Saxon kings, then of the earls of Cornwall. It is of a squarish figure, not very large, environed with a high wall and deep ditch. There is a rampire [sic] of earth within, equal in height to the top of the wall at present and makes a terrace walk overlooking the city and country. … In this place is the assize house and a chapel.[56]

The medieval guildhall was drawn with great care: its frontage is similar to that depicted by Ichabod Fairlove in 1709. The perspective is that from the southern side of High Street. Pinnacles are shown at the top of the portico though these were thought to have been removed in 1718.[57] The Custom House sits within a busy quay area. To the far right stands the warehouse, while alongside it and above are the Quay and Water Gates. The Custom House had at this time open ground-floor arches. Before this building was erected in the 1680s the city's custom houses had been located in a variety of locations including Topsham and in Cathedral Close at what was later Mol's Coffee House.[58] In 1698 one visitor discovered that the custom house had:

> an open space below with rows of pillars, which they lay in goods just as its un-laden out of the ship in case of wet. Just by are several little rooms for land waiters, etc., then you ascend up a handsome pair of stairs into a large room full of desks and little partitions for the writers and accountants – it was full of books and files of paper. By it are two other rooms, which are used in the same way when there is a great deal of business.[59]

The quay has considerable detail including three ships, barges and row boats. The Quay Gate stood below Water Gate. Both were demolished in the early nineteenth century.

Two other buildings, Bedford House and the Bishop's Palace, are less easily distinguished from surrounding buildings. The former had been a Dominican friary, converted by the first Earl of Bedford in 1539, but was pulled down in the 1770s to make way for Bedford Crescent (later Bedford Circus). It is now the site of the Princesshay Shopping Precinct.[60] In 1700 one visitor thought little of Bedford House. He wrote: ''tis large enough for a duke but makes no show, standing backward. And indeed has no show to make being very indifferent.'[61]

The Bishop's Palace is difficult to distinguish from a clutch of buildings around the cathedral. A thirteenth-century building, it would be rebuilt in the nineteenth century but in 1743 it retained more of its medieval character.

In the early 1700s two impressive buildings were built in Exeter, but only one could be depicted by Birchynshaw: the new hospital, described as 'The Infirmary', had recently been erected in Southernhay. The foundation stone was laid on 27 August 1741, and it opened a year and a half later. The building would later be known as Dean Clarke House. The two principal promoters were Alured Clarke, dean of the cathedral, and John Tuckfield, a merchant and later Tory MP. On the day the foundation stone was laid thousands of Exonians watched a long procession of gentlemen wind its way from the Chapter House through St Peter's Churchyard and into Southernhay. One commentator noted: 'every heart was full of joy too great to be expressed... such a day of gladness has not been known here for many years'.[62]

The second building, omitted by Birchynshaw because it lay too far from the city, was the workhouse. Built more than a generation earlier, it served all of the city's parishes and was situated on a large site, which is now occupied by Waitrose on Heavitree Road. In 1700 an East Anglian commented upon the building works:

> half a mile out of Exeter there is a hospital or rather a work-house about building to employ the poor, built wholly at the charge and by the contrivance of the Presbyterians, because the others would not encourage the undertaking, which was too great a discredit to the last and too great an honour for the first, and in order to the building of it, they burn the brick upon the place, which afford a soil for that purpose, though tis a nasty one, being a dirty red, yet such as all the houses twenty miles and more about that place are built with, but look nastily, I must tell you for I thought it looked very prettily and I never saw the like afore, that each kiln took up at least half an acre of ground, and when once used, they made a new one, and the whole contrivance is very pretty but too tedious to give you or myself the trouble of a description of.

It opened the following year and survived until the Blitz of 1942.[63]

Birchynshaw also identified in his plan four other buildings. These comprise the serge market in the midst of South Street and the corn market, now the Corn Exchange, located on the south side of the top of Fore Street. The former appears to have been erased from the map, leaving only a note to indicate its location. The selling of serge was, according to Daniel Defoe in 1724, 'a wonderful thing, well worth a stranger's seeing'. The corn market was later described as a 'quadrangular building supported by wooden pillars'.[64] The third building was St John's Hospital, established as a boy's school more than a century before, which was situated at the top of High Street near East Gate. A fourth building, Bradninch, was not placed in the modern location of Bradninch Place but between the castle and Gandy Street, where the Phoenix stands today.[65]

It would be misleading to regard Exeter as looking medieval in 1743; the late sixteenth and seventeenth centuries had been a period of robust rebuilding and renovation. Buildings rose in height and leaned over the streets: tall gabled buildings were commonplace. These ranged from the mid sixteenth-century 41 & 42 High Street (now occupied by Laura Ashley) to 16 & 17 Cathedral Yard (now the Well House), which were rebuilt and heightened in the late 1600s. Buildings in a more classical style could also then be seen such as the custom house, 5 Cathedral Close (now ASK) and 40 High Street (now Skechers).[66] These were built of brick, a material not in use in Exeter for frontages until about 1700. As a number of insurance policies drawn up at this time attest, some houses were built partly of brick in the early 1700s. For instance, one of the buildings depicted by Birchynshaw outside North Gate would have been that occupied by John Cadbury, a serge-maker, in 1736. His slate-roofed dwelling house was made of brick, cob and timber. Another serge-maker, Francis Robins, had a brick and timber house in Preston Street in 1743, while below him outside the West Gate lived Christopher Burnett, a tucker, in a similar house. Two houses, completely made of brick, were occupied by Richard Croker, a fuller, in the parish of St Martin in 1727. One of these was 57 High Street, situated across from the Guildhall.[67]

The Reformation had also fundamentally changed the medieval cityscape. In the 1530s St Nicholas Priory, like the Dominicans' friary, had been converted for domestic use. Other buildings, used as Exeter townhouses by priors and abbots or by cathedral staff, had likewise been converted. This included buildings that eventually became the Royal Clarence Hotel, the Well House and Mol's Coffee House.

Exeter's two graveyards are also clearly shown by Birchynshaw. That for Holy Trinity Church, consecrated in 1664, is seen across from the Royal Devon & Exeter Hospital, and the second, in Friernhay, was established in 1637. It was noted as 'Bartholomew Church Yard'.[68] Individual tomb graves are shown in both sites.

The cleanliness of the city was not so easily depicted. In about 1746 one Exonian claimed that it was 'securely, healthily and pleasantly situated on the sides of a hill'. Later commentators would dispute his assertion about the hygienic nature of the streets, but he then wrote further that: 'a brisk shower or two of rain, at least with very little aid of broom and shovel, prove[s] its natural scavengers, scouring away its filths, as divers torrents drive, with hurtless precipitation, quite down to the river'. He quoted Jonathan Swift's poem 'A Description of a City Shower' because he felt it was relevant to Exeter. The materials in the waves of filth comprised: 'sweepings from butchers' stalls, dung, guts and blood, drowned puppies, stinking sprats, all drenched in mud, dead cats and turnip tops, come tumbling down the flood'.[69]

Birchynshaw also drew 'the shambles' otherwise known as Butchers' Row, which had been in existence by then for more than two centuries. It was described in 1806 consisting:

of a narrow street, the buildings in general low and mean, with heavy hanging window shutters. Here the knights of the steel reside in a kind of community among themselves, slaughter their cattle and expose their meat for sale… the slaughtering of cattle with the accumulation of dung, blood, etc. thrown in heaps behind the houses makes the Butcher Row a noisome [disagreeable] place in the summer.[70]

The refuse cascaded down Stepcote Hill to West Gate.

The greatest built feature of Exeter was its wall, which in 1743 was known to have Roman origins of nearly seventeen centuries earlier. Eight medieval towers were carefully depicted by Birchynshaw. Four appear between East and South Gates; these were, in order, the 'Hospital Tower', the 'Bedford Postern Tower', the 'Lollard's Tower' and an unnamed tower near Holy Trinity Church. Snayle Tower, situated at the north-west corner of the wall near Friernhay, was also depicted as were the three towers of Rougemont Castle: firstly, 'John's Tower' stands above Northernhay between the Sally Port and East Gate; secondly, 'Athelstan's Tower' is situated at the corner of the ditch with Northernhay; a third castle tower lies inside the city wall and above the castle ditch.[71]

The four main gates were drawn in some detail, although South Gate, with its two towers, is less successfully drawn than the others. The gates were demolished over a period of fifty years: North Gate (1769), East Gate (1784), West Gate (1815) and South Gate (1819). Each one had distinguishing characteristics. South Gate was used for many years as a prison and debtors' gaol; it was known for the room called The Shoe, from which shoes were dangled by debtors asking passers-by for alms. East Gate was ornamented by a statue of Henry VII and included a chapel. North Gate was latterly used as a public house and from the darkness of its rooms was termed 'Hell', while West Gate was distinguished for having been by far the least imposing structure.[72]

Birchynshaw managed to depict nearly 700 buildings inside the city walls and some 600 outside them. It was later calculated that at the end of the 1700s Exeter had a total of 3276 buildings. Many were in existence in 1743, but the city was losing its position as the largest urban area in Devon. It was being overtaken by Plymouth, which had Dock (later Devonport) established in the 1690s. The latter grew from a satellite settlement into a large and fashionable town. In contrast, Exeter was still largely confined within its ancient walls, although separate and distinct communities lay across the river in St Thomas and immediately outside the East, West, South and North Gates.[73]

The main roads in and out of Exeter were shown, although most of the names differ from those used today. These comprise Bristol Road (Sidwell Street), London Road (firstly, Paris Street and Heavitree Road and secondly, Magdalen Street), Plymouth Road (Alphington Street) and Barnstaple & Bideford Road (St David's Hill). Only Topsham Road continues as a modern street name. Birchynshaw's map does not extend as far as the gallows at Livery Dole, where condemned prisoners were executed. In 1743 they would have included Reverend Peter Vine of Hartland who was found guilty not only of the rape of a child but also of the murder of the man sent to arrest him. A large crowd gathered to see the cleric hanged.[74] Exe Street, which runs below Mount Dinham, was noted as Exe Lane.

The principal streets and lanes within the city walls were also noted in the plan. Only a handful have retained the name given by Birchynshaw. These comprise Broadgate, Friars, Martin's Lane, Pancras Lane and Paul Street. Little Stile, which cut through from the top of South Street into Cathedral Yard, was in existence until just after the Second World War. Nineteen thoroughfares have different names. These are Arches Lane (Mary Arches Street), Bear Lane (Bear Street), Bedford Lane (Bedford Street), Castle Lane (Castle Street), Corry Lane or Gandy (Gandy Street), Fryerhay Lane (Friernhay Street), George Lane (George Street), Goldsmith Lane (Goldsmith Street), Idle Lane (King Street), Little Britaine (Bartholomew Street), Milke Lane (Market Street), Mint Lane (The Mint), North Gate Street (North Street), Prestern Street (Preston Street), Rack Lane (Rack Street), Rocks Lane (Coombe Street), South Gate Street (South Street), Stick Lane (possibly The Arcade) and Waterberry Street (Waterbeer Street). Some public ways are unnamed, including Catherine Street, Frog Street, Longbrook Street, Parliament Street, Quay Lane and West Street.

River features such as the quay, Exe Island and Exe Bridge were drawn. Exe Island was the area outside the walls between Upper Leat and the river. Its ownership had been disputed with the Courtenay family for hundreds of years before it was granted to the city by the crown in 1550. The island was not only a highly industrial part of Exeter but also densely populated. The bridge was then more than five hundred years old and had some seventeen arches. Not all are visible on the map. Houses are depicted on both ends of the bridge as well as the Church of St Edmund to the east. The bridge was replaced in 1770 by a new bridge, which was built a short distance upstream. The arches over the main Exe were demolished but the eastern remnant, with the church and houses, was retained and eventually became known as Bridge Street. The houses were taken down in the early 1880s and the church was demolished in 1972.[75] The leat system is depicted in some detail: both Higher and Lower Leats are shown as well as a weir and several bridges. Powhay, Cuckingstool, Cricklepit and Lower Mills are also depicted. The water-processing building below Mount Dinham was noted as the `Water House'. This had been erected nearly thirty years previously to enable wooden pipes to bring water to a large cistern behind the Guildhall. In 1698 it held:

> 600 hogsheads of water which supplies by pipes the whole city. This cistern is replenished from the river which is on purpose turned into a little channel by itself to turn the mill and fills the engine that casts the water into the trunks which convey it to this cistern.[76]

Society

The people who inhabited the city drawn by Birchynshaw were then being chronicled by Andrew Brice, the Georgian inheritor of the Elizabethan John Hooker, who was also Exeter's first historian. Brice had been born in 1692 and was the son of a shoemaker. His commentary on Exeter appeared from 1717 in his own newspaper, *The Postmaster*, as well as in *The Mobiad*, a mock-heroic account in verse of the election of 1737, and in the *Grand Gazetteer* for which the lengthy article on Exeter was written in 1752.[77]

There were some 14,000 people living in Exeter in 1743. Brice may have been aware of the conclusions one visitor had made in 1724 of them. He had written:

> The people are industrious and courteous: the fair sex are truly so, as well as numerous; their complexions, and generally their hair likewise, fair. They are genteel, disengaged [free from obligatory connections], of easy carriage and good mien.[78]

Almost 30 years later Brice himself described his fellow Exonians. He compared many 'of our well-bred' with a well composed' bowl of punch. 'Merry Andrew', as he was called, felt some were overly acidic, in others there was too much spirit and a third group he considered to be like water because he found them insipid. He approved of their dress sense, which he thought suited a trading city; these men and women dressed in a comely and genteel fashion without resorting to being 'gaudily foppish'. Brice thought that their social diversions were not financially ruinous and he noted they supported winter concerts. He also commended the 'middle sort of tradesmen', the 'artificers and handicrafts-men' and the 'very meaner people' who lived in Exeter. In general he thought that the latter were better behaved than their London counterparts. In Brice's opinion they were not 'quite so rude, rugged, licentious, ferocious, riotous and disturbing'.[79]

Even so, Brice was not without some minor criticisms. He reported that the lane leading up to Rougemont Castle was infamous for 'drabbing', that is, prostitution, and compared it to Damnation Alley in Plymouth. He also deplored the use of the walls of St Lawrence's Church as a public urinal. Brice conceded that its church tower was barely taller than the chimneys of domestic houses and related the tale that when a country boy had first seen the tower he cried out to his mother, 'Look, look, Mother, what a *gurt chimley* that little house hath got!'[80]

High Street was the main thoroughfare, and in 1750 it was commented: 'it is surprising to see how the great street is filled on market day with people and great plenty of all sorts of provisions'. Nine years earlier a Cornish traveller regarded it as 'very handsome'.[81] Exeter drew in Devonians from across the county. It was the cultural capital, although theatre-going was impeded by the city council in the 1740s. It actively prosecuted actors on charges of vagrancy. Councillors regarded plays as having corrupting influences on the morals of the city's youth. The theatre was situated behind the guildhall in Waterbeer Street and was closed by the council in 1745. A few years later there were attempts to circumvent the council's policy of not allowing public performances in unlicensed premises by arranging for admission through the sale of packets of tooth powder instead of paid tickets.[82] In comparison, plays were freely performed across the river, and thus beyond the control of the city council, in the parish of St Thomas. *The Beggars' Opera*, for example, was offered at the Seven Stars Inn.[83]

Exonians had been gathering in the city's coffee houses for business and pleasure since the 1670s. In 1743 there was Mol's and Will's in St Peter's Churchyard as well as Lewis Jones' in High Street. Travelling exhibitions could be seen in the Apollo Room at the New Inn, the city's largest inn. Exonians also gathered for social events in other inns such as the Bear in South Street, the Half Moon in High Street and the Oxford Inn outside East Gate.[84]

Exeter benefited because it was also Devon's centre of religion and justice; the diocese was run from the bishop's palace and the Assizes met at Rougemont Castle, where in the spring of 1743 seven prisoners were sentenced to be executed. Three men had been convicted of stealing horses, another for forgery, a fifth man for stealing a sheep, another man for murdering his wife and finally a woman for the inhuman murder of her apprentice maid'.[85] Details of the circumstances of three of the prisoners were reported. The forger was:

> John Lawford, condemned for uttering and publishing a false note in the name of Bennet & Company, bankers and goldsmiths in London, for £300. He was possessed of a pretty good estate, having married a wife with a handsome fortune, whose father was a colonel of the militia in London. He was born in Wiltshire, aged 54. Great interest was made to save him but in vain. He was to have been executed at six in the morning but was at length obliged to go in the cart with the other malefactors. He behaved very bold (as the World terms it) and breakfasted on coffee and bread and butter before he went to execution. And wore in the cart his boots and a gold laced hat. This unhappy man has left behind him four children, and his wife very big with child, under inexpressible affliction.

The woman who was convicted was:

> Alice Stribling, aged about forty, condemned for the murder of her apprentice maid, occasioned by striking her on the head with a stick, of which she died in about five hours after. Her behaviour, while under sentence of death, was very sullen. Her husband is a farmer and lives in good repute in the parish of George Nympton.

David Gibbons, a man aged about thirty, was also found guilty of murder. He testified:

> at the time this melancholy scene happened, he found her in a very indecent scene upon the floor, very much disguised in liquor, as he thought, and endeavoured to lift her up, being assisted by a woman then present with no other intentions (as he declared upon the words of a dying man and hoped for salvation) then to take all necessary care of her. That he was in the utmost confusion at the time he said was very true, and that he did push her from him with some violence and she fell to the ground, which grieved him and he again helped her up but whether her death proceeded from a fall or was occasioned by a fit, he called upon God to witness he did not know, for that he never struck her all the time, though she expired in a few hours. It seems she had only a small wound upon her nose, which could not occasion her death.[86]

Newspapers were printed earlier in Exeter than in most English cities. By 1704 the city's residents could read editions of *The Exeter Postman*, and seven years later Brice's newspaper appeared.[87] Brice was in competition with the Farley family who also had a newspaper in Bath, Bristol and Salisbury. *The Exeter Postman* had been started by Samuel Farley, and in 1740 his nephew Edward was imprisoned for selling newspapers illegally. Members of their family were also charged in Exeter with sedition on two other occasions.[88]

In the early 1740s newspapers printed in other parts of the country, both in the capital and in the provinces, often reported Exeter's news. These were often otherwise unrecorded in Exeter itself. This includes such stories as the freezing of the river in January 1740: 'A sheep was roasted whole upon the ice above Exe Bridge, where were present many hundred spectators.'[89] Likewise, there was a fire in 1741:

> there was a dreadful fire there on Tuesday night last, which burnt with such violence that had there been any wind, it would have endangered half the city but it happened to be very calm and only burnt three houses near Mr Foster's wine cellar.[90]

Other accounts were longer, such as that which reported disease in 1741:

> for several days a terrible distemper raged amongst the people, of which great numbers have died; and out of four physicians in that town, three are already dead, and the other so dangerously ill that his life is despaired of.

but secondly:

> We hear from Exeter, that at the Assizes there was such a sickness among the prisoners, that half were not able to appear upon their trials; and those that did, were brought to the bar single, having first been stripped of their clothing, washed all over with vinegar, and then fresh clothes put on them.[91]

That summer a tragic report of a visit to Bellair, now part of Devon County Hall, was printed:

> Last Friday night Mr Pagge, a Swedish young gentleman, who resided [as] a merchant in this city, for his general deportments etc. [was] well esteemed, having been on a rural visit with J. Deur of Bellair, Esquire in the latter's chaise, on their return, near St Magdalene's [sic] in our suburbs, it being dark and the way rugged, the coachman by a violent shock was thrown off the box. On which the horses taking fright ran away so precipitously wild that the gentlemen in their consternation imagining it safest to jump out, Mr Deur did so, with no greater mischief than a strain, but his misfortunate friend, by a wheel passing over, had his right leg shattered in a miserable manner. The fractured bone was set by a skilful surgeon; but a mortification attending the wound, the broken limb on Sunday was cut off above the knee. But all the care possible was defeated; for the gangrene spread so irresistibly that he expired on Wednesday morning and was at night interred in our cathedral.[92]

Perhaps one of the strangest appeared across the country in August:

> an elderly gentlemen of a good estate in that neighbourhood was poisoned by his own children. Tis said that his cruel usage made them unanimously come to a resolution to commit so rash an action in order to rid themselves of the slavery they underwent.[93]

Economy

Exeter was not just the social and cultural focus of an extensive hinterland that stretched into western Dorset, southern Somerset and the far reaches of West and North Devon. It was also the centre of a regional cloth trade, which in 1743 still underpinned Exeter. It has been estimated that four people out of five earned their livelihoods in the woollen cloth industry.[94]

Daniel Defoe famously noted in 1724 that Exeter was a city 'full of gentry and good company, and yet full of trade and manufacturers also'. It lay at the hub of an important heartland; from the countryside came vast quantities of woollen cloth, which was shipped from the Exe to European markets. By 1743 cloth had been the city's economic mainstay for at least four centuries,[95] and the industry is one of the most prominent features of Birchynshaw's map: the racks on which the cloth was dried are shown not only along the river in the Bonhay, at Mount Dinham, on Exe Island and Shilhay but also higher up on the Friars. One commentator noted in 1750 that:

> Without the South Gate on the spot of the Priory of Grey Franciscans is a great manufacture of narrow cloths and shalloons extending all the way down to the river and the cloths when they are hung up make a very beautiful appearance. This place is called The Friars.[96]

The racks were commented upon by other visitors including in 1700 by an East Anglian who enthused:

> We went to the place where their racks stand, as they call them, for stretching and drying their serges and kersies, a commodity that prevails more here than in any city in England besides and is well worth a stranger's sight.[97]

By 1743 the industry had undergone tremendous changes in regulation, types of cloth, materials, production techniques, skills and in the markets in which they were sold. The dominant cloth had become serge, with perpetuanas becoming the favoured type. The term had been in use since 1601,[98] but it took several generations to rise into pre-eminence. Local wool supplies were augmented by imports from Ireland, Wales and Spain. From the 1720s onwards Irish yarn began to replace Irish wool. In 1757 a local gentlemen recalled:

> I very well remember to have seen large droves of horses laden with wool-packs almost daily passing our road, going from Minehead to Tiverton and other trading places, which I was told was Irish wool and I have been informed that at those times, which was in the years 1746 to 1752 or thereabout, there were 1,500 to 2,000 packs of wool yearly brought over from Ireland to Minehead.[99]

Cloth production involved employing thousands of workers; children and women were spinners but women were also burlers while the men were sorters, combers, weavers, fullers, pressers, shearmen, dyers' labourers and packers.[100] In 1753 it was calculated that the city had 119 serge-makers, combers and weavers. This figure was part of an analysis of voters, which recorded a total of 1537 freeman eligible to cast a vote. The author of the report tabulated voters by occupation (see Table 1).

Table 1: Exeter Freemen by Occupation, 1753

Point-makers, Pipe-makers & Horners	5
Chair-makers & Basket-makers	9
Masons	13
Cork-cutters, Painters, Cutlers & Brasiers	14
Saddlers	17
Mariners, Husbandmen & Labourers	22
Undistinguished by Trade	32
Helliers (Tilers or Slaters)	42
Smiths & Tinplate-workers	45
Glaziers, Dyers & Coopers	49
Barbers	50
Carriers, Fellmongers (dealers in hides), Glovers & Skinners	51
Butchers	52
Druggists, Apothecaries & Grocers	62
Bakers, Hatters & Chandlers	67
Tailors	95
Joiners & Carpenters	100
Gentlemen, Merchants & Goldsmiths	103
Fullers & Pressmen	110
Serge-makers, Combers & Weavers	119
Cordwainers	133
'Promiscuous' [indiscriminate] Trades	144
Total	1,537

By his calculations cloth-workers were some fifteen per cent of the freemen in Exeter; other cloth-workers were dyers, fullers and pressmen.[101] To this should be added the many hundreds, if not thousands, of cloth-workers who were not eligible to vote.

Attempts were made in the early 1700s to form friendly societies or clubs, the predecessors of trade unions. In 1717 a military officer at Exeter wrote to the government requesting guidance. He wrote:

> The journeymen weavers in this place and in the neighbouring towns, under pretence of hard usage from their masters, assemble themselves after a notorious manner in great bodies, sometimes to the number of 300, sometimes more, having a captain at their head and although the Act against riots has been read to them they laugh and despise it, insulting both the magistrates and all other persons that refuse to join them, pulling down houses and taking serges out of merchants' shops. They have proceeded so impudently in this town as to give me petitions desiring the regiment to stand neuter, pretending extraordinary zeal for his Majesty's Service.

In 1718 and again in 1726 the city council petitioned the government against this activity, which included demands for a minimum wage. Subsequent legislation banned 'unlawful combinations' of cloth workers.[102]

Exeter's cloth was produced in the countryside and market towns, such as Crediton, Cullompton and Tiverton, before being sent to the city where it was finished. A national publication noted in 1744 that Exeter's trade had declined:

It has always been a place of great trade and is so at present, as well as the whole county but it is generally apprehended there is not now so much commerce nor the manufacturers so fully employed as formerly. However, it is hoped that such vicissitudes, both here and in other parts of the kingdom, will not fail to excite the attention and when the industry of all those who can anyways contribute to promote what may justly be called the vital motion of Old England.[103]

The years from 1670 to 1720 were the city's 'Golden Age' of cloth production and when the chief markets were the ports in the Netherlands and to a lesser extent those in the Baltic, in France and in other Continental countries. At this time Exeter's cloth accounted for a quarter of all English sales. The following decades, from 1720 to 1750, saw a contraction in the industry owing to two factors. Firstly, Norwich merchants replaced those of Exeter in selling cloth not only in Spain and Portugal but also in the Netherlands. Exeter also had competition from Yorkshire merchants who likewise undersold Devon cloth in the English home market.[104]

The first few years of the 1740s were particularly difficult for Exeter's cloth workers. In November 1740 it was reported that the industry had 'decayed' throughout the West Country. One report claimed that 'many thousands of those people in the neighbourhood of Exeter are out of work and scarce any are employed in that large and populous county'.[105] The loss of sales continued, and in 1745 trade was reported to be at a standstill because of the threat of a French invasion.[106]

It was during 1743 that two eminent merchants died. An Exonian only identified as a Mr 'Thorn' died in December. He was described as having been 'esteemed the greatest cloth maker in England'. No details have been found for him.[107] A few months before John Colsworthy of Mount Radford had died. He was described in the *Derby Mercury* as 'a person of great note amongst the Quakers. His corpse was carried in a hearse, attended by 13 coaches, to the Quakers' Burying Place, and there interred in a very handsome manner. His wealth, amounting to £20,000, he has left among his children.'[108] At this time the best-known of the city's cloth merchants was Johann Baring who had emigrated from Bremen in 1717 and a few years later married into a prosperous Exeter merchant family. By the time of his death in 1748 the Baring family had become one of the wealthiest cloth-makers in Devon and went on to be national bankers.[109]

The disruption in the 1740s was caused initially by the outbreaks of war with Spain in 1739 and with France in 1744. Markets closed and foreign privateers captured Exeter ships. Local merchants complained of their ship losses, but what is perhaps most surprising is a report sent from the city in 1746:

> All day yesterday a very smart engagement was fought off Budleigh between some English and French Men of War, which made the houses shake all along the coast. We heard the firing at Heavitree and Exeter. I could distinguish Broadside and Broadside in my grounds, though nine miles from the sea. The fire continued till between 10 and 11 at night, when the firing ceased; but it began again this morning at 4. The success on either side is uncertain; but late last night three loud huzzas was heard by a gentleman coming over Haldon from on board the ships.[110]

Transport in and out of Exeter was difficult for a number of reasons. A considerable portion of cloth reached overseas markets through Exeter's canal, a sixteenth-century innovation to overcome weirs on the Exe. It had been extended in the late 1690s, and in 1700 a visitor watched the work. He commented:

> they had then made a very great progress and are likely in a short time to complete it and without any great charge, for their method is to put the minister and chief inhabitants of each parish upon encouraging the working people (in hopes of a future advantage) to go voluntarily in, which they daily do five hundred at least, and are carried down every morning by a minister and his chief parishioners with drums and trumpets etc. and liquor all which so enlivens them that they strive who should go oftenist and who should do most when they come there.[111]

The county's roads were notorious. By 1743 Exeter had a long history of utilising pack horses for transporting goods via its difficult network of ancient roads but wagons were increasingly used. They took a week to reach London. Travellers walked, rode on horses or used stage coaches, which brought passengers to London in four days during the summer and in five during the winter months.[112]

The largest coastal import was coal from Wales and the North East of England, while from foreign ports came linen and canvas (Germany, the Netherlands and Belgium), wine, fruit, salt, dyes and cork (Spain, Portugal and the Canaries), tobacco, sugar, rice, rum and naval stores (the West Indies and North America) and cured fish and fish oil (Newfoundland).[113]

Not surprisingly there were ancillary businesses and trades to the cloth industry. Perhaps one of the more unexpected was horticulture. Exeter became known for garden nurseries in the nineteenth century, but one of the most prominent had been established in 1720 by William Luccombe. It developed into a considerable business through the nineteenth century. His principal achievement was introducing the 'Lucombe Oak'. A traveller noted this in 1776 while on a visit to the nursery:

> I was entertained for an hour very agreeably, viewing a great variety of fruit and forest trees with which his garden abounds being a nursery. Here I saw the live oak, a species of the evergreen originally raised by this man from the Leghorn iron oak. Tis in great esteem, makes a handsome tree growing up very straight and much greater than the common oak.[114]

Luccombe's interests were varied, and another achievement has gone unrecognised. Twelve years after the drawing of Birchynshaw's map Luccombe raised pineapples at his nursery. It was reported in a newspaper:

> We have this week seen here a curiosity, very great in itself as being a rarity, but more so on account of its uncommon cultivation. The same is the luscious rich fruit, proper to the hot East Indies, and some warm parts of America, called the *Ananas*, and by us, for its resemblance to the cones of pine trees, the pine-apple. It is still more ripening on its strange sort of plant and is the property of Mr Luccombe, the very ingenious and industrious gardener, at Bowhill House, in St Thomas's and was raised by him (a thing before imagined impracticable) not in a hot house or bark mould &c and yet, to as great a degree of perfection as any hath been in England, in the Gardens of the *Virtuoso*, by the said hot cultivation. Some or other article of our *Topographical Dictionary* holds a description of it and we might give such here, for the satisfaction of those who never read it, but that the truly curious may go and view it more satisfactorily with their own eyes. We may well call it a rich and luscious fruit, the pulp whereof dissolves in the mouth, when we are assured by those who have enjoyed its charming relish, that its taste seems a Commixture of the Muscadine Grape, a mature Quince, and the finest peach and hath divers virtues. Mr Luccombe, if I mistake not, hath divers more now growing in the same manner; which seems to me to be a considerable point attained in the Art of Gardening.[115]

It is difficult to discover Exeter's level of interest in African slaving, as it is with most of Devon. There had been three voyages more than a generation earlier: the *Betty* of Exeter had sailed to Cape Verde in 1698; the *Dragon* of Topsham had voyaged to Africa in 1699; and the *Daniel & Henry* of Exeter and Dartmouth sailed for Guinea in 1700. The accounts of the latter ship show that London merchants supplied most of the trade goods for which the Africans were subsequently purchased. The voyage was a financial failure and lost nearly £1500 for its investors. It may have been because of this that the next such ship to leave Exeter did not sail for more than fifty years. In the eighteenth century there were only three voyages: these sailed in 1757, 1760 and 1762. Another twenty-two ships voyaged from Devon for slaving during this period, and this number included eleven French vessels. A total of between 4128 and 4193 such voyages had sailed from British ports.[116]

Government

Exeter was governed in 1743 largely in the same way as it had been for centuries. Twenty-four men controlled the city; they comprised sixteen common councillors and eight aldermen who administered Exeter, as the Chamber, in the room over the entry porch of the Guildhall. The latter also acted as the city's magistrates. These men were self-selected; upon the death of one of their number the remaining twenty-three chose a replacement. Many remained in post for decades.

The office of mayor was an annual appointment made at Michaelmas. Nicholas Medland, who lived in the parish of St Petrock, had been elected in 1742 and continued until September 1743. Like many of his predecessors since the Reformation, he was in trade. Also like all of the others since 1688, Medland was an Anglican; by law Dissenters were forbidden from being a member of the Chamber. Wealth and family connections were additional factors and members of the Chamber were most likely to have been Tories. Medland was a druggist, one of the five occupations from which nearly three-quarters of the council were drawn.[117] In September 1743 Philip Elston was elected. He was an eminent goldsmith, an occupation from which a high number also became mayor.[118]

Exeter's mayoral elections had two hallmarks; one was the ceremonial nature within the Guildhall but the other was the mob violence in the streets. The antics were described by Andrew Brice, Exeter's illustrious newspaperman, in his *Mobiad* otherwise known as *The Battle of the Voice*. This was his 'heroic-comic poem, sportively satirical, being a briefly historical, natural and lively, free and humorous description of an Exeter election'. It was composed in 1738.

Brice intended to hold up to public inspection Exeter's contemptible election practices; he hoped Exonians would 'be ashamed of the ridiculous or base parts which they, as if [they] were in effigy, review [how] they acted in the wretched farce'. Brice wanted to stir consciences. In 1737 the rival mobs adopted cockades, one in blue to show support for the Tories while the others sported yellow for the Whigs. Dirt, filth and dead cats were among the materials thrown at electoral rivals. The violence was enhanced by the Exeter practice of 'quilling'. This system of supplying hospitality, in the form of food and alcohol, to voters and members of the mob was not confined to Exeter but the city had coined its own word to describe the practice.[119]

The party political nature of the dispute led to factions inflating the number of voters, the freemen. This occurred in both mayoral and parliamentary elections. In 1735, 1736 and 1741 the elections for mayor were particularly boisterous, and in the latter year two Tories were elected Members of Parliament. They remained in office for the following six. In 1727 a seat was held by a Whig, and seven years later both seats had been taken by the party. The Chamber responded by packing the body of freemen with 240 honorary freemen 'composed of the most zealous gentlemen, clergy, and attorneys of the Tory party'. This ensured their victory in 1741, but it was hotly contested. It was reported that autumn:

> From Exeter we hear, that they have been in so great confusion in that city, that two persons have been imprisoned, and the proclamation against riots has been read by the magistrates before the tumult could be suppressed, raised on account of the making some honorary freemen with a view to the approaching election; a method always indulged by persons in the court interest, if 'twill possibly serve their turn; but sorely galling, if used by the contrary side.[120]

In 1753, and possibly in other years, the Whig supporters evaluated each of the city's 1537 freemen on their political allegiances. Each man was recorded in one of seven categories; there were 'good', 'bad', 'doubtful', 'queries', 'abroad or as far from home as London', 'alms' or 'abjure'.[121] The successful candidates nearly always came from one class: from 1713 through to 1776 every one of the city's MPs, with one exception, was drawn from leading county families.[122]

Elections might have been relatively straightforward had the city been divided only between the majority of the freemen who supported the Tories, whose supporters were Anglicans and had strong allies in the cathedral, and the Whigs who were drawn from the Dissenters. However, in 1743 there remained in Exeter strong memories of the suppression of Monmouth's Rebellion of 1685 and the march three years later through the streets of William of Orange who had brought his Glorious Revolution. The third disruptive force in the city was Jacobitism, which dogged Exeter through the early 1700s.

Jacobitism, or accusations of it, periodically appeared in Exeter and was associated with the Tories. For instance, in 1704 it was reported that Sorrel, the horse which contributed towards the death of William III, had been brought to Exeter where it received a warm welcome from supposed Jacobites. One Exonian, who served the mayor as his swordbearer, was, reportedly, so friendly that he kissed the horse. A leading cathedral official toasted the horse with claret. Nine years later, in March 1713, the city erupted in celebration when restrictions on the anti-Whig and allegedly pro-Jacobite preaching of Dr Henry Sacheverell expired. Church bells were rung across Exeter, although not those of the cathedral. Guns were also fired from the city walls, a procession marched through the streets and bonfires were lit including at the deanery in St Peter's Churchyard. Lancelot Blackburne, one of Exeter's most colourful deans, was a particular target of the Jacobites, and there was an attempt on the deanery with fire. This was one of the most unusual attacks on a city building. It was concluded by:

> five or six of the female zealots [who] did with great modesty pull up their coats before the men, and discharged their lower tier of guns, which were fully loaded, against the gate, to batter it in *breech* while others fetched a barrel of the like ammunition to finish the storm.[123]

Blackburne was a supporter of the Hanoverians and his worldly reputation, including gossip about his moral laxity and having been a buccaneer, suggests that the dean would not have been overly shocked by the alleged behaviour of a handful of Exeter women.[124] The rioters were also refused permission to light a bonfire in front of the cathedral. Interestingly, Bishop Offspring Blackall's reputation among his contemporaries was that he was distinctly high church.[125]

The accession of George I in 1714 was, at least according to the city's official history, greeted with great joy in Exeter. However, an independent observer noted that on the day of the king's coronation rioters attempted to break windows and attack dissenters' meeting houses.[126] Fears of a Jacobite invasion led one commentator to advise the national government that there was little support in Exeter for a revolt. He discounted reports that the Tories had set in place organised support among the working population.[127] Nevertheless, four years later a Topsham man was reported to have said 'God Damn King George', and a similar charge of sedition was levelled shortly afterwards against an Exeter newspaperman for printing a scandalous letter against the king. He served nearly a year in prison. In 1733 it was a grenadier who was punished for disloyalty to the king. He had toasted the Pretender's Health with the title of King James the Third. On two successive days he received three lashes from each of his fellow soldiers and was then 'drummed out' of Exeter with a halter around his neck. It was intended that the lashes would be severe enough to kill him, but three fellow grenadiers were thought to have been unenthusiastic; they themselves were given twenty, thirty and fifty lashes. Jacobite support rumbled on in Exeter through to 1745 during the invasion of Scotland and northern England.[128]

Religion

In 1742 Exeter had a new bishop and dean but neither of the men lasted long in their posts nor did they appear to have made much of an impact. Bishop Nicholas Clagett, described by one biographer as having been 'conscientious and methodical', died in 1746, and Dean William Holmes, a former Regius Professor of History at Oxford, died two years later.[129] Of Clagett another biographer noted, 'little else is recorded of him' other than his death.[130]

There was more notable activity among the Dissenters. Nearly a century before Birchynshaw's map Exeter had all of its parish churches closed except four (St Edmund, St Mary Arches, St Mary Major and St Petrock), and the cathedral was divided into two parts by a brick wall in order to provide separate worship for the Independents and the Presbyterians.[131] By 1743 two generations had passed since the return of the Anglicans to their parish churches and cathedral. A number of meeting houses were opened for the Nonconformists.[132] According to a survey of Anglican parish clerics in 1744 there were, within the city walls, fewer than two thousand Dissenters in a population of some ten thousand. It is probable that there was underreporting of non-Anglicans; the figures were noted in many instances as estimates (see Table 2).

Table 2: Non-Anglicans in Exeter in 1744

	Families	Presbyterians	Arians	Baptists	Quakers	Roman Catholics	Jews
All Hallows (Goldsmith)	26	3	-	-	2	-	1
All Hallows (Walls)	107	36	-	-	1	-	
Holy Trinity	357	95	-	4	7	-	
St Edmund	350	3	2	-	1	-	
St George	94	16	-	2	1	4	
St John Bow	72	15	-	-	2	-	
St Kerrian	40	5	5	3	-	1	
St Lawrence	50	-	-	-	-	-	
St Martin	57	6	-	1	-	-	
St Mary Arches	80	9	-	-	-	-	
St Mary Major	412	75	8	6	1	2	
St Mary Steps	200	4	-	-	-	-	
St Olave	134	13	-	-	-	-	
St Pancras	31	1	-	-	-	-	
St Paul	51	5	-	-	-	-	
St Petrock	55	12	6	2	-	1	
St Stephen	56	5	-	-	-	-	
Total	2172	304	21	18	15	8	1
Total (4.5 persons per family)	9774	1368	94	81	67	36	4–5

The table shows some 16.5 per cent of the city's population were Nonconformists. To these figures could be added those Methodists who were active in Exeter by 1745. The cleric for Holy Trinity referenced the Methodists in a note that in Mr Kennedy's house 'Mr Whitfield and his brethren assemble the mob and pretend to teach and expound the scriptures'. There was also a Presbyterian Meeting House in each of the parishes of Holy Trinity, St George and St Kerrian, a Quaker Meeting House in Holy Trinity, an Arian Meeting House in St Olave and a Baptist Meeting House in St Mary Major. The Quaker Meeting House lay outside the city walls at Wynards. There was also a congregation of forty French Protestants who worshiped at St Olave's Church.[133]

Exeter's generation after 1743 witnessed a resurgence of the cloth trade, a continual splintering of the Dissenters, a decline in the city's national standing, a continued fear of French invasions and the unexpected loss of the North American colonies. The city also entered into an Age of Improvement during which Exeter was partly modernised. This did not extend to its form of government; it was not until the 1830s that the Chamber was forced to reform its seventeenth-century administration. Exeter may not have fallen asleep in the nineteenth century but it was at least heavily dozing through to the Second World War. By then, the city looked back to itself in the early 1700s, at the time when Birchynshaw drew his map, and saw this as having been its Golden Age.

Fig. 27. Exeter Guildhall, as engraved for John Rocque, 1744

Fig. 28. (above). The river Exe, from the west bank looking upriver to Exe Bridge, as engraved for John Rocque, 1744

Fig. 29. (left). The north wall of Rougemont Castle, with Northernhay, seen from across the Longbrook Valley, as engraved for John Rocque, 1744

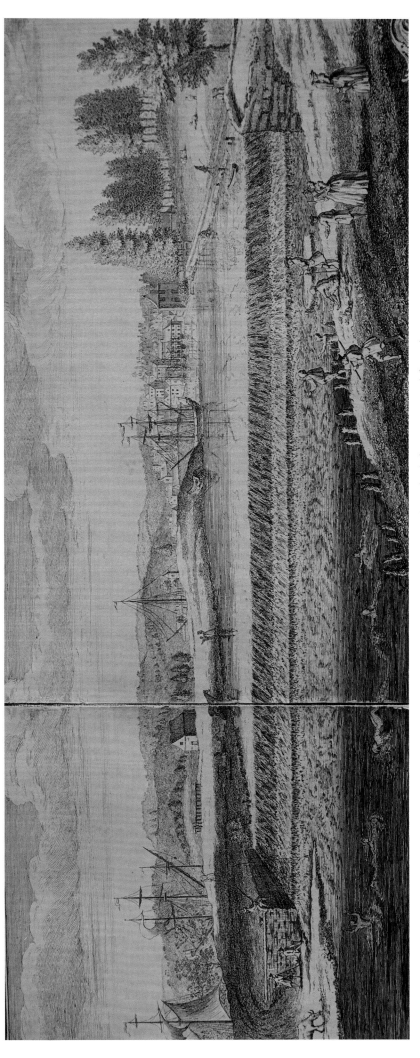

Fig. 30. Trews Weir on the river Exeter, looking upriver to the Custom House and with the canal on the left, as engraved for John Rocque, 1744

Fig. 31. The west side of the Royal Devon & Exeter Hospital, later renamed Dean Clarke House, with a burial taking place in the graveyard of Holy Trinity Church, as engraved for John Rocque, 1744

Fig. 32. The workhouse as engraved for John Rocque, 1744

Fig. 33. View into Cathedral Yard, with the cathedral in the far distance and the Church of St Mary Major to the right, as engraved for John Rocque, 1744

Fig. 34. View from Martin's Lane and Catherine Street looking towards the cathedral, with the Treasurer's House on the left and the Church of St Mary Major on the far right, as engraved for John Rocque, 1744

Fig. 35. The former city hospital in Paris Street as engraved for John Rocque, 1744

Notes

1   For introductions to early urban cartography in Britain, see Roger Kain and Catherine Delano-Smith, *English maps: a history*, London: British Library, 1999, 180–216, and Roger Kain and Richard Oliver, *British town maps*, London: British Library, 2015. The Catalogue of British Town Maps accompanying *British town maps* is at https://townmaps.history.ac.uk/, and the 'CBTM' numbers in these notes refer to this catalogue.

2   An introduction to this is K. M. Constable, 'The early printed plans of Exeter 1587–1724', *Report and Transactions of the Devonshire Association,* LXIV (1932), 455–73, but he was not aware of the important Fairlove map of 1709. A more recent cartobibliography of Exeter is Francis Bennett and Kit Batten, *The printed maps of Exeter 1587–1901: 300 years of Exeter history*, Exeter: Little Silver Publications, 2011. This lists 63 distinct maps with notes on variant states and issues and illustrations of most of the maps listed.

3   For Hooker, see William Ravenhill and Margery Rowe, 'A decorated screen map of Exeter based on John Hooker's map of 1587', in Todd Gray, Margery Rowe and Audrey Erskine, *Tudor and Stuart Devon: the common estate and government*, Exeter: University of Exeter Press, 1992, 1–12; our account of Hooker is based on this, unless otherwise noted.

4   This was published as Walter J. Harte, J. W. Schope and H. Tapley Soper, *John Vowell, alias Hoker, The Description of the Citie of Exeter*, Devon & Cornwall Record Society, II–III (1919) and I (1947).

5   Hooker's map is CBTM 20603.

6   Constable, 'The early printed plans of Exeter', 456.

7   Constable, 'The early printed plans of Exeter', 459–61, suggested that the first state was a proof; Ravenhill and Rowe, 'A decorated screen map', 3–4, note the inept treatment of the compass.

8   Ravenhill and Rowe, 'A decorated screen map', 3.

9   The screen is discussed by Ravenhill and Rowe. The manuscript map is CBTM 22835, and is in a volume of town plans in the British Library, apparently produced in France in the mid-seventeenth century; the British examples evidently derive from Speed, and tend to show very little detail inside city walls.

10   Roger Kain and Catherine Delano-Smith, *English maps*, 104. Speed's map of Exeter is CBTM 18419.

11   Sarah Bendall, 'Draft town maps for John Speed's *Theatre of the Empire of Great Britain*', *Imago Mundi*, 54 (2002), 30–45.

12   CBTM 18254.

13   CBTM 18750.

14   CBTM 18302. There is some doubt whether the Exeter and other maps should be attributed to Merian, or his son Matthias Jr, or to Beer: see D. Smith, 'The enduring image of early British townscapes', *Cartographic Journal*, 28 (1991), 163–75 (esp. p. 169), and Raymond Frostrick*, The printed plans of Norwich* (2002), 19.

15   CBTM 18749. For Izacke, see T. N. Brushfield, 'Richard Izacke, and his "Antiquities of Exeter"', *Report and Transactions of the Devonshire Association*, XXV (1893), 449–69.

16   CBTM 21160.

17   CBTM 18305.

18   Constable, 'The early printed plans of Exeter', omits all mention of the map.

19   CBTM 18266.

20   Brian Robson and David Bower, 'The town plans and sketches of William Stukeley', *Cartographic Journal*, 53:2 (2016), 133–48. Stukeley's map of Exeter is CBTM 18306.

21   Laurence Worms and Ashley Baynton-Williams, *British map engravers*, London: Rare Book Society, 2011, 156.

22   The map only came to light in the summer of 2018, and was thus too late to be included in CBTM.

23   There are references to Thomas Birchinshaw at Tiverton in 1733 and 1741, and to John Birchinshaw at Ottery St Mary in 1762: https://www.foda.org.uk .

24   This spire – probably actually a pyramid roof – was removed in 1752–3.

25   Devon Heritage Centre, ECA, Act Book 14, 3 April 1743.

26   John Varley, 'John Rocque: engraver, surveyor, cartographer and map-seller', *Imago Mundi*, 5 (1948), 83–91.

27   CBTM 18290.

28   There is actually some doubt about the scales used by Rocque: it is possible that, rather than 1:2400, he actually used the common estate-survey scale of one inch to three chains, 1:2376. There is a difference of about one per cent between these two scales, which is less

than the distortion to be expected in printing from copper: in order for the ink to 'take' the paper was wetted, and then dried afterwards, causing shrinkage. Scale-distortion can be further affected by subsequent mounting on textile or other materials.

29   CBTM 22338.

30   Plate 8 in *A collection of plans of the principal cities of Great Britain and Ireland...*, London: A. Dury, n.d. [1764]: CBTM 18389.

31   CBTM 18242.

32   Benjamin Donn, *A map of the county of Devon 1765*, reprinted in facsimile with an Introduction by W. L. D. Ravenhill, [Exeter:] Devon and Cornwall Record Society, NS 9 (1965), 16.

33   CBTM 18255.

34   Worms and Baynton-Williams, *British map engravers*, 743.

35   No example is known in a public collection.

36   CBTM 18256.

37   CBTM 22899: f.p. [1] in Alexander Jenkins, *The history and description of the city of Exeter and its environs, ancient and modern...*, Exeter: P. Hedgeland, London: Longman, etc., 1806. Top centre on the map is 'Engrav'd for Alexr. Jenkins's History of Exeter'.

38   CBTM 18239.

39   Brian Robson, 'John Wood 1: the undervalued cartographer', *Cartographic Journal*, 51:3 (2014), 257–73 and Brian Robson, 'John Wood 2: planning and paying for his town plans', *Cartographic Journal* 51:3 (2014), 274–86.

40   The Exeter map is CBTM 18312.

41   Brian Robson lists 15 – including one in Jersey – which are not in the CBTM database.

42   CBTM 18731.

43   CBTM 18257: originally published in R. Montgomery Martin, ed., *The Illustrated Atlas and modern history of the World*, The London Printing and Publishing Company, n.d.: the British Library copy was accession-stamped in August 1851.

44   CBTM 18740: in *A handbook for travellers in Devon and Cornwall*, 5th edition, London: Murray, 1863, f.p. 17: the map was reused unaltered in *ibid*, 6th edition, 1865, p. 7, and 8th edition, 1872, f.p. 2.

45   The following is mostly based on J. B. Harley and J. B. Manterfield, 'The Ordnance Survey 1:500 plans of Exeter, 1874–1877', *Devon and Cornwall Notes and Queries*, XXXIV (1978), 63–75.

46   Harley and Manterfield, 'The Ordnance Survey 1:500 plans', 69.

47   Harley and Manterfield, 'The Ordnance Survey 1:500 plans', 63.

48   Harley and Manterfield, 'The Ordnance Survey 1:500 plans', 74, in n.27, citing Exeter Streets Committee minutes, V, 524.

49   John Ogilby, *The Traveller's Guide* (1712), 35; Laurence Echard, *The gazetteer's or newsman's interpreter* (1744); *Magnae Britanniae Notitia* (1743), 10.

50   Todd Gray, *Exeter Travellers' Tales*, Exeter: The Mint Press, 2000, 39.

51   Gray, *Exeter Travellers' Tales*, 39.

52   Andrew Brice, *The Grand Gazetteer*, Exeter: Andrew Brice, 1759, 544; Todd Gray and Sue Jackson, *St Martin's Island*, Exeter: The Mint Press, 2017, 115.

53   *Joseph Bliss's Exeter Post-boy*, 4 May 1711.

54   Exeter Cathedral Library & Archive, D&C3568, p484. I owe this reference to John Allan.

55   Gray, *Exeter Travellers' Tales*, 42.

56   Gray, *Exeter Travellers' Tales*, 43.

57   S. R. Blaylock, 'Exeter Guildhall', *Devon Archaeological Society Proceedings*, 48 (1990), 153; *Exeter Guildhall*, Exeter: Exeter City Council, 2000 edn), 23.

58   Todd Gray, *Exeter Unveiled*, Exeter: The Mint Press, 2003, 65–7.

59   Gray, *Exeter Travellers' Tales*, 33.

60   W. G. Hoskins, *Two Thousand Years in Exeter*, Exeter: J. Townsend, 1960, 137; Gray, *Lost Exeter*, 66–7.

61   Todd Gray, *Garden History of Devon*, Exeter: University of Exeter, 1995, 39–40; Gray, *Exeter Travellers' Tales*, 39.

62   Alexander Jenkins, *The History and Description of the City of Exeter*, Exeter: P. Hedgeland, 1806, 203–5; Robert Newton, *Eighteenth Century Exeter*, Exeter: University of Exeter, 1984, 26; 'An account of the Devon & Exeter Hospital', *Gentleman's Magazine*, 11 (1741), 474 and 497.

63   Gray, *Exeter Travellers' Tales*, 40.

64   Joyce Youings, *Tuckers Hall Exeter*, Exeter: University of Exeter, 1968, 158; Gray, *Exeter Travellers' Tales*, 47; Jenkins, *Exeter*, 388.

65   The place name goes back to at least 1290: Devon Heritage Centre, ECA, Mayor's Court Roll, 18–19 Edward I.

66   Gray and Jackson, *St Martin's Island*, 12–24.

67 Stanley D. Chapman (ed.), *The Devon Cloth Industry in the Eighteenth Century*, Exeter: Devon and Cornwall Record Society, NS 23 (1978), 55, 60, 65, 68.

68 Brice, *Grand Gazetteer*, 544.

69 Brice, *Grand Gazetteer*, 540.

70 Jenkins, *Exeter*, 388.

71 Mark Stoyle, *Circled With Stone; Exeter's City Walls, 1485–1660*, Exeter: University of Exeter, 2003, 20–7.

72 Todd Gray, *Exeter Engraved; The Secular City*, Exeter, 2000, 46–75; *Western Times*, 3 March 1849.

73 W. G. Hoskins, *Devon*, Newton Abbot: David & Charles, 1954, 527, 530, 114–15; Newton, *Eighteenth Century Exeter*, 112–13.

74 *General Evening Post*, 23–26 April 1743; *Derby Mercury*, 28 Oct. 1743.

75 Stewart Brown, *The Medieval Exeter Bridge, St Edmund's Church, and Excavations of Waterfront Houses, Exeter*, Exeter: Devon Archaeological Society, 2019, 100; Gray, *Exeter Unveiled*, 56–9; Todd Gray, *Lost Exeter*, Exeter: The Mint Press, 2002, 2–9.

76 Walter Minchinton, *Life to the City*, Exeter: Devon Books, 1987, 20–3; Gray, *Exeter Travellers' Tales*, 33.

77 Ian Maxted (23 Sept. 2004). Brice, Andrew (1692–1773), printer. *Oxford Dictionary of National Biography*. Retrieved 18 June 2019, from https://doi.org/10.1093/ref:odnb/3379; *Exeter Flying Post*, 4 Jan. 1849.

78 Newton, *Eighteenth Century Exeter*, 3; Gray, *Exeter Travellers' Tales*, 42.

79 Brice, *Grand Gazetteer*, 549–51.

80 Andrew Brice, *The Mobiad*, Exeter: Andrew Brice, 1770, 50–1, 53.

81 Gray, *Exeter Travellers' Tales*, 54, 50.

82 Todd Gray, *Not One of Us*, Exeter: The Mint Press, 2018, 46.

83 Newton, *Eighteenth Century Exeter*, 24.

84 Newton, *Eighteenth Century Exeter*, 24, 20; Gray, *Exeter Unveiled*, 66.

85 *London Evening Post*, 24–26 March 1743.

86 *London Evening Post*, 23–26 April 1743.

87 https://bookhistory.blogspot.com/2009/10/devon-newspapers-1704-2004.html .

88 *Caledonian Mercury*, 24 June 1740; *Ipswich Journal*, 28 June 1740; *Report on the Records of the City of Exeter* (1916), 246; Gray, *Not One of Us*, 155–6; Ian Maxted (3 Jan. 2008). Farley family (per. 1698–1775), printers and publishers. *Oxford Dictionary of National Biography*. Retrieved 18 June 2019, from https://doi.org/10.1093/ref:odnb/64308.

89 *London Evening Post*, 15–17 Jan. 1740.

90 *London Evening Post*, 9–11 June 1741.

91 *Newcastle Courant*, 4 April 1741; *Stamford Mercury*, 9 April 1741.

92 *London Evening Post*, 9 June 1741.

93 *London Evening Post*, 16–18 Aug. 1743.

94 W. G. Hoskins, *Industry, Trade and People in Exeter*, Manchester: Manchester University, 1935), 53.

95 Gray, *Exeter Travellers' Tales*, 47; Maryanne Kowaleski, *Local Markets & Regional Trade in Medieval Exeter*, Cambridge: Cambridge University Press, 1995, 19–20.

96 Gray, *Exeter Travellers' Tales*, 55–6.

97 Gray, *Exeter Travellers' Tales*, 39.

98 Ben Johnson, *The Fountain of Self Love* (1601).

99 Hoskins, *Industry, Trade and People*, 31–2; *Gentleman's Magazine*, 27 (1757), 59.

100 Hoskins, *Industry, Trade and People*, 52.

101 University of Nottingham, Manuscripts & Special Collections, Ne, C535.

102 National Archives, SP35/10, fo. 41; Youings, *Tuckers Hall*, 108–9.

103 Hoskins, *Industry, Trade and People*, 12; *The Geography of England* (1744), 47–8.

104 Youings, *Tuckers Hall*, 86–8, 167–70; E. A. G. Clark, *The Ports of the Exe Estuary*, Exeter: Exeter University, 1960, 112.

105 *Ipswich Journal*, 1 Nov. 1740.

106 *Gentleman's Magazine*, Vol. 13, 1743, 139; *Stamford Mercury*, 10 Oct. 1745.

107 *Ipswich Journal*, 31 Dec. 1743.

108 *Derby Mercury*, 25 Aug. 1743.

109 S. Kelly (23 Sept. 2003). Baring [née Vowler], Elizabeth (1702–1766), wool manufacturer and merchant. *Oxford Dictionary of National Biography*. Retrieved 28 Mar. 2019, from http://o-www.oxforddnb.com.lib.exeter.ac.uk/view/10.1093/ref:odnb/9780198614128.001.0001/odnb-9780198614128-e-53256.

110 *Caledonian Mercury*, 19 May 1746.

111 Gray, *Exeter Travellers' Tales*, 39.

112 Newton, *Eighteenth Century Exeter*, 19–20; *The Exeter Pocket Journal* (1750), not paginated.

113 Hoskins, *Industry, Trade and People*, 62–5.

114 *The Magic Tree: Devon Garden Plants*, Exeter: Devon Books, 1898), 17–18; Andrew Oliver (ed.), *The Journal of Samuel Curwen, Loyalist*, Cambridge, MA: Harvard University Press, 1972, II, 262.

115 *Andrew Brice's Old Exeter Journal or the Weekly Advertiser*, Jan. 1755.

116 Todd Gray, *Devon and the Slave Trade*, Exeter, 2007, 43–56.

117 Newton, *Eighteenth Century Exeter*, 36–41; Exeter Cathedral Library & Archives, VC21983 & VC21979.

118 *London Evening Post*, 1–4 Oct. 1743; J. F. Chanter, 'The Exeter Goldsmith's Guild', *Report and Transactions of the Devonshire Association*, XLIV (1912), 464–7, 477–8.

119 Brice, *The Mobiad*, ii, xv; Newton, *Eighteenth Century Exeter*, 26; Gray, *Not One of Us*, 31, 155.

120 Romney R. Sedgwick, 'Exeter, 1715–1754', in Sedgwick (ed.), *The History of Parliament: the House of Commons, 1715–1754*, Woodbridge: Boydell & Brewer, 1970; *Ipswich Journal*, 13 and 20 Sept. 1740.

121 University of Nottingham, Manuscripts & Special Collections, Ne, C535.

122 Hoskins, *Industry, Trade and People*, 20.

123 Gray, *Not One of Us*, 154; *The Flying Post*, 4 April 1713.

124 Andrew Starkie (3 Jan. 2008). Blackburne, Lancelot (1658–1743), archbishop of York. *Oxford Dictionary of National Biography*. Retrieved 27 Mar. 2019, from http://o-www.oxforddnb.com.lib.exeter.ac.uk/view/10.1093/ref:odnb/9780198614128.001.0001/odnb-9780198614128-e-2516.

125 Andrew Starkie (28 Sept. 2006). Blackall, Ofspring (bap. 1655, d. 1716), bishop of Exeter and religious controversialist. *Oxford Dictionary of National Biography*. Retrieved 27 Mar. 2019, from http://o-www.oxforddnb.com.lib.exeter.ac.uk/view/10.1093/ref:odnb/9780198614128.001.0001/odnb-9780198614128-e-2507.

126 Todd Gray, *The Chronicle of Exeter, 1205–1722*, Exeter: The Mint Press, 2005, 161; Jenkins, *History*, 200.

127 National Archive, SP35/15, fo. 181.

128 Gray, *Not One of Us*, 30, 32, 111–12, 154–8; National Archive, SP35/42/2, fo. 41, 6 April 1723; *London Evening Post*, 27 Nov. 1733.

129 M. Watkins (4 Jan. 2008). Clagett, Nicholas (1685/6–1746), bishop of Exeter. *Oxford Dictionary of National Biography*. Retrieved 27 Mar. 2019, from http://www.oxforddnb.com/view/10.1093/ref:odnb/9780198614128.001.0001/odnb-9780198614128-e-5425; Exeter Cathedral Library & Archive, D&C3567, 197–200 and D&C3568, 201–2.

130 George Oliver, *Lives of the Bishops of Exeter*, Exeter: William Roberts, 1861, 162–3.

131 George Oliver, *The History of the City of Exeter*, Exeter: privately printed, 1884, 118–20; Brockett, *Nonconformity*, 11–12.

132 Brice, *Grand Gazetteer*, 540.

133 Alan Brockett, *Nonconformity in Exeter, 1650–1875*, Exeter: Exeter University, 1962, 114–15, 59–60.

Index

DEVON AND CORNWALL
RECORD SOCIETY PUBLICATIONS

Previous volumes are available from Boydell & Brewer Ltd.

A Shelf List of the Society's Collections, ed. S Stride, revised 1986

New Series